You Can Sing If You Want To

by the same author

Cleo

You Can Sing If
You Want To

Cleo Laine

VICTOR GOLLANCZ
LONDON

First published in Great Britain 1997
by Victor Gollancz
An imprint of the Cassell group
Wellington House, 125 Strand, London WC2R 0BB

A catalogue record for this book is available from the British Library.

ISBN 0 575 06355 6

Designed and typeset by Production Line, Minster Lovell, Oxford
Printed in Great Britain by
Hillman Printers (Frome) Ltd

97 98 99   5 4 3 2 1

This book is dedicated to Liz Knights,
who sadly died before its completion.

Acknowledgements

With my special thanks to John Dankworth for all his patient help. Many thanks also to Sheila Gray, Becky Stevenson, Avril Dankworth, Faith Evans, David Gray, Sara Holloway and Liz Knights.

Contents

Prologue: You Can Sing If You Want To 9

Section I: Prepare Your Body

1. Is that a Vocal Class? 14

2. Let's Get Meditative 17

3. Good Breathing Habits 19

Section II: Train Your Ears

4. I Cannot Hold a Tune 26

5. More About Intervals 32

6. You've Got Rhythm? 39

Section III: Practice Makes Perfect

7. Interpretation 48

8. Sound 56

9. Establish a Routine 63

Section IV: Songs to Practise On 70

Section V: The Pleasures and Pitfalls of Performing

10. Showing Off Your New-found Skills 82

11. The Alchemy of Acoustics and Amplification 86

12. Care of the Voice 95

Section VI: A Personal Perspective

13. A Musical Background   102

14. Breaking into the Profession   106

15. Teachers and Role Models   116

Questions and Answers   121

Epilogue: Good Luck, All You New Songbirds!   124

Useful Names and Addresses   126

Prologue

You Can Sing If You Want To

If you talk, hum, la–la–la, at any time in your daily routine, at work or at play, you should – unless you have a hearing or vocal problem that needs medical attention – be able to learn how to sing.

Most people do sing at some time or another – while doing the house-work, say, or in the shower or bath – perhaps to alleviate boredom or drudgery or simply for the feeling of joy it gives. Some people sing Christmas carols or hymns in large congregations when they assume that no one is paying attention and noticing what a ghastly, out-of-tune noise they are making.

It's coming out in the open as a soloist that scares the living daylights out of many would-be singers, whether their secret vocal ambitions are professional or amateur. Yet in my experience, with a concerted effort of practice and thought, most aspiring singers are capable of producing a pleasant sound, a sound they could show off with confidence – the key word.

The need to sing seems to be on a great many people's minds, whether they are young or old. It is a natural longing for most people, probably because it is one of the most direct forms of self-expression. During my long career as a professional singer I have met and talked to thousands of aspiring singers who have one big fault: lack of confidence in their ability, which makes them timid about getting up to perform. Though they are not alone, they think they are.

Delving deeper, I have found many reasons that could account for this lack of musical self-assurance, when in other areas of their lives, confidence abounds. The main reasons people have given me are that music was never played in their house, or that any effort at musical expression was denigrated.

The desire to sing has also been stultified in a flat-dwelling society, which has to consider the neighbours living above or below. Most young children, from a very early age, love to sing and dance noisily. It's such a happy experience for them, discovering all the new and raucous sounds and movements they can make with abandon. Anything that comes out they enjoy – if left to enjoy. But for a lot of little ones, there is a mum with a headache or a dad on night work to contend with, when what they need are large fields, big houses or neighbours who don't give a damn, so that what comes naturally from their voices is not suffocated before it has a chance to develop.

Another reason for not singing that I hear over and over again is that people were told it was not a career option when they asked for lessons. Well, it doesn't have to be a career option. Just singing for the mere pleasure of it is the most wonderful reason. It's uplifting, good for your lungs, and therefore good for your general health and well-being.

So there you have a whole slew of reasons that put potential singers off singing. One of them may be yours. Or perhaps you have a real killer in your closet that's all your own.

Let's get rid of it now.

The true voice that has been hidden for years can come out in the open if you wish to reveal your secret desire to let fly. You're never too old to have a go, and if you're young you should be singing already anyway – out loud, wherever and whenever you feel like it. Now is the time to discover that reasonably good singing voice you have always wanted, the one you can show off with confidence.

There are a few singers who, for inexplicable reasons, can do very little wrong and just need guidance from a second pair of ears. For some reason the gods put everything in the right places for them – I call them the 'soarers to the heights'. Then there are those who have the equipment but need a little help to get it to 'soar' for them. After those two categories come many degrees of delightful sounds, from the charmingly soft and beautiful to the gruff and entertaining whisky-laden styles. Some professionals with such sounds earn a good living, and others are millionaires. But the great majority of people who sing are amateurs who do it for the pure joy and release the experience gives them. What we all had in common – career singers and amateurs – was the initial desire to sing.

At what level do you think you could sing if given the chance? There is always a starting point for any objective (which is to improve what you have). So first of all, start to listen carefully to the sound and style you are producing now, without putting yourself down, so that you can begin with an assessment that is as honest as possible of the kind of voice you have at this moment.

It does mean you must start singing out a little more and listening hard to yourself whenever you sing. If you do this and really work at the exercises that come later in this book, you will be able to review the level that you gave yourself at this starting point. Later, you may well want to give yourself a pat on the back for the way your sound has advanced. You will hear, as the weeks pass, that you are singing better. Don't expect immediate miracles though; improvements take time, practice and determination, and what you hear eventually will depend on the amount of time each day you gave it.

You have now brought into play one of a singer's greatest assets – your ears! The more you become determined to start using them as never before, the more you will benefit from this book and from any singing lessons you take now or in the future.

Throughout this book the part of your head most frequently mentioned will be your ears. If you are not a natural listener – to conversation, nature and sounds in general – now is the time to start training your ears to listen to things going on around you. Be aware of as much as you can. Don't let music or talking on the radio wash over you like canned music. Listen, listen, listen.

When you listen to recordings of your favourite singer, start thinking about what it is that you like about that voice. Be more critical. Start listening to the instruments that are accompanying the singer, pick out one and concentrate on it – choosing the one you might have a hankering to play may help you to concentrate. Try to do this as many times as you can, and take in the arrangement as well as the singer. You will be starting to train your ears to listen.

If you don't already have one, buy a tape recorder. This will be the other important piece of equipment that you must learn to use constantly. Make it another part of your body, record yourself warbling wherever you are and listen to the results. It will give you many surprises, from those first, startling, 'Oh my God – is that me?' sounds, to the pleasing renditions later (or earlier, if you already had an agreeable voice but had not listened to it). I think a lot of you will be pleasantly surprised. You never hear yourself as others do, but a tape recorder does help to make clear to you the assets as well as the negative qualities that need to be worked on. So make that first recording. Sing a simple song – simply, gently, with a range that is comfortable and natural for you. You may hear, to your ears, a sound you dislike, or you may have a confidence breakthrough just doing it. I will try to boost your confidence further or help you to acquire the sound you're after.

Everyone has a unique, thumbprint voice that depends on their physique – the shape of their head and chest and throat – and also on their personality. All they have to do is discover it. I'm not saying you will turn out to be a Pavarotti, Sinatra, Sutherland or Fitzgerald. But you never know – you may turn out to be the first you!

Section I

Prepare Your Body

1

IS THAT A VOCAL CLASS?

Singing involves the whole person and is done best when energy is flowing – indeed, some styles require an immense amount of energy. It is also one of the purest forms of self-expression, and part of singing is using your imagination and allowing it to take flight. To do this you need a clear head and a relaxed body. This became apparent to me when I was a tutor at the Wavendon AllMusic Courses. The evenings at the courses were wonderful social occasions, with all kinds of music and singing. Some vocal students would stay up late, maybe also drinking and smoking, and would turn up to the morning class in no condition to put their minds to singing or discussing any approaches for improvement.

When I was confronted with these singers, who had literally dragged themselves out of bed to attend a singing lesson, I realized something more than humming was needed to wake them up and get them ready to sing. I devised a plan to start them on their day's work – whether they felt like it or not. So – windows were flung wide open and in came the chill April air.

'Right, everybody. Up on your tiptoes – slowly. Now lift arms above head – slowly does it.'

'What about my high heels?'

'Kick 'em off!'

So you, too: go up on your toes and raise your arms. If you are not used to such a balletic movement as balancing on your toes, do the best you can – or just stand solidly – but raise your arms and take in a good breath through the nose, then slowly, slowly, expel the air through your mouth, while lowering your arms to your sides. Repeat the movement several times.

Slowly raise your arms out to the sides again. At the same time, gradually rise on to your toes, try to keep your balance and continue raising your arms until they are straight up by the sides of your ears, then slowly lower your arms and feet. Breathe in while you are going up and out while coming down. Repeat three times.

Now bend over from the hips like a rag doll. Flop, as if you have no muscles or bones to hold you together. Flop, hang, head down, the only thing you can do successfully is breathe; all other muscles have gone flop – head, neck, shoulders; arms swing, fingers flap, knees are bent. You feel like a jelly – enjoy the feeling. Tip your pelvis up, tuck in your bot, round your back, feel the stretch and slowly, knees bent, roll back up. And again. Bend over from the hips like a rag doll. Flop, relax all your muscles, from head to toe, be like jelly. Enjoy the feeling, for a slow count of eight, tip your pelvis towards your navel, your bottom tucked under, round your back, enjoy the stretch. Slowly, knees bent, roll up, one vertebra at a time. Repeat again. And if you need it and like it, do the jelly roll again, slowly.

Letting it all hang out at Wavendon

Another good exercise to loosen things up and remove any inhibitions is the musical whirl. For this, I usually put on a record that has given me much enjoyment – a record that not only makes me happy but also makes me want to move to it. I tend to sing along in unison with the theme and the improvisations the musicians play. Put on your own favourite piece of music, then let your imagination take flight. You might find that instrumental music will fire your imagination the most, but it's your taste in music that does the trick – vocal, guitar, saxophone, trumpet or orchestras galore. Move to the music being played in any way that you feel inspired to at the moment; if it conveys to you gentle swaying, then sway; if you want to jump for joy, then go for it. Be as creative as your imagination allows you to be – go down any path the music wants to take you.

When you do this exercise regularly, and as you become more familiar with the music, sing along with it. If you hear a line of music being played that stands out for you, and suits your range, then use your ears and try to copy what you're hearing, whatever it is. But open your mouth, make a noise, sing – softly, gently, angrily, humorously, loudly. Let rip! If you do it with a friend or a group, don't be swayed by what your neighbour is doing or get embarrassed by the sound coming out of their mouths. Do your own thing, in your own time, but do it. When I did this exercise with my class at Wavendon, you can't imagine the sounds that came through the open window – not to mention the gyrating bodies of all ages: some of the more extrovert ones got quite wild. A horn tutor passing by the window one morning exclaimed: 'That? That is a vocal class?'

The singers greatly looked forward to the daily morning awakening and releasing. I also discovered that a smattering of musicians, drawn initially by the music, shyly joined us to loosen themselves up for the day, ridding themselves of the cobwebs collected the previous night.

The music does not have to be fast and furious – slow movements are as valid as any other – as long as you get moving and singing along with it. If someone walks in and catches you at it, invite them to join you. Combine the breathing, the jelly roll and the musical whirl as a daily exercise. You will soon notice a difference in your vitality, and if you put on a piece of music you think you could never learn in a million years, you will be surprised – eventually you will get to know it by heart.

2

LET'S GET MEDITATIVE

As I hope the previous chapter made clear, singing is a physical activity, and it is hard to do well if you are stiff or tense. Before we start the exercises in this chapter, make sure the jelly roll has relaxed your shoulders and neck: your shoulders should be loose and down. Now stand confident and tall, with a happy, smiling face.

Have you ever had a good hum?

If you have, you know how to produce that sound. But let's get a little more adventurous, adding 'oh' to start the 'mm'. Now I want you to sustain it for as long as you comfortably can on one breath. It should make the sound that a monk makes in a Buddhist temple, when he joins in with the others to meditate.

The aim is to get a good sustained humming sound that vibrates the lips and head like a bee buzzing around your ears: 'Oohmmmm.' Try to imitate that bee sound, without tensing up – as you might if a bee happened to be buzzing around you. But you are the bee, so it's all quite natural for you to 'Oh-m-m-m-m, oh-m-m-m-m, oh-m-m-m-m'.

'What do I do to relax? I have no idea how to go about it.' I've often heard this plea from singers. Actually consciously tensing what is already tense – in other words, exaggerating a tension to sigh it away – is one way of solving the problem. If you find yourself tensing, stop and open your mouth as wide as possible. Then really tighten all the muscles in your face and neck – even stick out your tongue and make yourself look gruesome – then flop back into place again, shoulders down, until the tension disappears. Relaxing for many can be such a mystery or worry, but now you know how to achieve it. Use these exercises whenever you feel tense.

Off you go again: 'Oh-m-m-m-m, oh-m-m-m-m, oh-m-m-m-m-m.' You can do this as many times as you wish, softly at first, increasing the volume as you become more relaxed and the sound flows naturally, 'Oh-m-m-m-m, oh-m-m-m-m, oh-m-m-m-m, oh-m-m-m-m'.

As you get to feel happy 'Ohm-ing' away to yourself, start making more of the vowel sound 'Oh'. Be comfortable, find a pitch you can manage with ease, then make 'Oh' a little more important, like the beginning of 'home'. Hold on to it for a couple of seconds, before you relinquish it for the 'm-m'. This may mean you will have to take a deeper breath to keep going, but don't panic. Take your time and your breath easily – if it runs out, it runs out. If you feel tense, relax your jaw, face, neck, shoulders – every part of your body – by consciously tensing then letting everything go. Then start again. 'Oh--m-m-m-m, oh--m-m-m-m, oh--m-m-m-m, oh--m-m-m-m, oh--m-m-m-m.' Now you are getting somewhere you may not have been before, depending on the rating you gave yourself at the start. You are sustaining a note on 'Oh' for two seconds, which should now be extended to an extra two, along with the 'm-m'. Keep an eye on the second hand of your watch or count in your head one thousand and one, one thousand and two, one thousand and three, one thousand and four, while you hold 'Oh' again, using a comfortable pitch. Then slip into the 'm-m-m', sustaining for a further count of four seconds.

You are no longer a bee – you are starting to become a singer. Keep going; you know what to do if you feel unhappy or tense. Stretch, screw up all those muscles, then let go. Start again and enjoy the sensation of 'Oh' held for four seconds, then 'm-m'; repeat three or four times, or more if you're enjoying the feeling. When you feel a change is needed, switch to a different sound, the sound made by the vowel 'aw' as in autumn, doing exactly as you did with the 'Oh' in 'Oh-m' – 'Aw--m-m-m-m, aw--m-m-m-m, aw--m-m-m-m'.

Keep it as smooth and even as you can, and try to raise your pitch when you do a second round. You may have noticed that your tongue lies at the back of the bottom teeth naturally and that the teeth are slightly apart. That's how it should be. If it's not like that, start doing it now – it all helps to keep you relaxed as you journey on to the next vowel sounds, 'ah' as in father, then 'ee' as in – would you believe it – bee.

These exercises will relax you, open up your throat and generally limber up your voice. The more you do them, the stronger your voice will get.

3

GOOD BREATHING HABITS

In singing – as in sport, playing a musical instrument, or any other activity that needs calm, control, endurance, relaxation and strength – healthy breathing is absolutely vital. People need to breathe more deeply than they normally do, to support and improve their chosen hobby, profession or physical exercise. Those who don't participate in any physical exercise at all on the whole use just the top part of their lungs, which gets them through their daily movements, until they are asked or forced to exert themselves suddenly. Then, lots of unused parts of their bodies, including the lungs, could give them a bit of a problem.

If a singer is not aware of the need to breathe, to use the maximum capacity of the lungs when it's necessary, then he or she can be likened to a sports car trying to win a race with inferior petrol in its tank or dodgy sparking plugs.

If you are a swimmer and regularly do several laps of the Australian Crawl, you are in good breathing company with many a famous singer. Legend has it that the long phrases achieved by Frank Sinatra in his illustrious career can be attributed to his having held his breath for several laps under water after a dive, which by all accounts gave him his great breath control. You don't have to go that far unless you want to. There are other ways to achieve good results that will help you sing better, and at the same time give you a feeling of well-being.

Breathing exercises should be done every day, if possible in an airy room, or outside if the weather permits (or with the window open if there isn't an outside to go to!). I know that, life being what it is, sticking to a daily programme might not be possible. But just being aware that it's important to improve your breathing habits and to practise whenever you have a free moment is a good beginning. So get into your loosest and most comfortable clothes, and tell everyone who might disturb you not to. Relax and give yourself up to the first of many breathing sessions, lying on the floor.

There is a lot to take in here, so go over it several times before you have your first session on the floor. Some of it may come to you without thinking – as everyday breathing should – which will give you a head start. But there will also be times when nothing will work for you. Don't despair if this happens, for if just one of the exercises falls into place for you it will be a plus for your singing. Everyone goes through a period of one step forward and two steps back before there is a break-through – but you learn such a lot about yourself along the way. When you eventually feel comfortable doing the breathing exercises lying on the floor, you can start doing them standing up, with your straight, relaxed posture. Gradually, with time and practice, everything will fall into place, without your having to think about what to do next when you sing.

This should be a calming time, listening to and observing what happens to your body, doing something that should come quite natu-rally but has to be re-learned or found again for singing. There is and always will be a wide difference of opinion (mainly from the operatic side) on how to go about it. When Birgit Nilsson was asked 'Is it dangerous to take too much breath before singing?' she replied: 'I have not been thinking too much about it; it should come easily and natu-rally. Of course, I know if I have a long phrase, I have to take a long breath.' Shirley Verrett worked hard at her breathing. 'People used to think my breath would go on for ever; they didn't know I had worked for years trying to compensate for a sway-back by taking difficult breathing exercises, reciting poetry . . . maybe a stanza or two in one breath . . . to compensate, to train the muscles.' Luciano Pavarotti takes a deep breath and stays in that position 'as when you are in the bath-room', as he delicately puts it, or you could 'push like a woman in labour, giving birth. When you push like that the diaphragm comes up'.*

* Quoted in Jerome Hines, *Great Singers on Great Singing*, Gollancz 1983.

Start by lying on the floor on your back, legs straight out, arms comfortably at your side, with your shoulders relaxed against the floor. If you have a sway-back, tilt your pelvis up to help close the gap between the floor and your lower back, and if you're still uncomfortable bend your knees. You will find that your body sinks into the floor sooner if you consciously relax for a few minutes. If you find yourself tensing, try the exercise we used in Chapter 1: stop and open your mouth as wide as possible and really tense all the muscles in your face, then let go.

Then apply the same technique for relaxing to the whole body, in much the same way that yoga has been taught for years. Starting from your toes, go quickly over your whole body with your mind, becoming aware of the muscles that are tense. It sometimes helps to close your eyes. Then concentrate on the toes of your right foot first; curl them down until they feel really tense, then release the tension and feel the sense of relaxation that it brings about. Don't rush it, be aware, listen and let the feeling take over and sigh away all the tightness. Now do the same with the whole foot – arch it back as hard as you can, tight and taut, then relax it and – oh!!! – give a long luxurious sigh.

As soon as you think you have got the idea, creep up your whole body, slowly switching from left to right, as you tense, relax and sigh, telling yourself at the same time that you are relaxed in your mind. Do not miss any spot on the way up, and when you get to your face you know what to do: grimace, open your mouth and tense everything – tight – tight – brow and forehead. If you need more, go back to the toes and start again. You may find it helpful to have a tape recording of these instructions playing, to guide you through each section of your body. Tapes can be bought on yoga, and some of them include this relaxation exercise. Once you are feeling comfortable you can start the breathing exercises.

Diaphragm
Put your hands on your tummy at the waistline, and inhale. Be aware of the in-and-out movement around the waist. This happens when the diaphragm (the part of the midriff that supports the voice) is used during inhalation, and it actually lowers into the abdominal area. Don't move the ribs in this part of the exercise.

Ribs
Place your hands so that they are supporting the sides of your lower ribs. Breathe in, taking care to raise only the rib-cage – don't tighten the tummy or the diaphragm. The waist will tend to go flat while you are performing this exercise because the tummy is sucked in as the relaxed diaphragm is raised upwards.

Combination diaphragm-rib
To maximize breathing capacity, both of the above movements must occur simultaneously. So now try to do them both at the same time. Experiment, trying to inhale so that the diaphragm moves down towards the feet (causing an outward movement at the waist) while the ribs move outwards, like the opening up of an umbrella. Gently does it.

Monitor your progress by putting one hand on the 'pyramid' area between the ribs and the other at the base of the ribs. The action of correct breathing should cause the hands to move outwards. Shoulders at all times should be well down – a million miles from your ears and quite relaxed.

Inhalations
- To gain control over the muscles of the ribs and diaphragm, inhale through your nose, retaining the breath and keeping the rib-cage expanded. Hold this position for a count of four, then breathe out. Exhale through the mouth, allowing the rib-cage to 'collapse'. Do this a number of times.
- Inhale through your mouth, imagining you are whistling in an inward direction, until you feel comfortably inflated. But never, ever overfill yourself. Hold for a slow count of four, then relax and expel the air through the mouth.
- Inhale deeply through the mouth, with quick, small yawns, filling up the chest. It should start low at the waist. As the air is exhaled, the ribs and the diaphragm should gradually relax.
- Draw in a supply of air by expanding the rib-cage, at the same time lowering the diaphragm and relaxing the tummy muscles. Open the mouth, permitting the air to enter the now vacant space in the lungs, an action not unlike a gasp of surprise – but don't overdo it! Expel the air by relaxing the diaphragm and ribs.

Exhalations

- To gain control of the muscles used in exhaling, imagine a feather on a table that you want to blow away. Inhale. Hold your breath for a count of three (not a slow count), then exhale through the mouth, relaxing the ribs in one movement, and try to move the feather with a quick burst of air.
- Imagine lots of feathers. Your aim is to blow them away with a long, controlled stream of air. Inhale, hold for three counts and remove all the feathers from the table with a gradual lowering of the rib-cage, paying close attention to the movements involved.
- Inhale deeply. Blow out the air very slowly and steadily, keeping the ribs completely open and motionless for as long as you can. Then, while continuing the exhalation, gradually allow the rib-cage to relax until at last you are at rest.
- Inhale deeply, then exhale in quick spurts, keeping the rib cage wide (using the abdomen to control your muscles, like going to the bathroom or bearing down). Do not inhale or exhale during the pauses between each spurt and keep your lips open. Doing a blow-pause, blow-pause pattern, practise until you get up to twenty spurts an inhalation without collapsing. Suspend the breath between spurts by keeping the ribs open. Inhale once more, trying for another twenty spurts. You should have noticed that as you are producing the small spurts of breath you use small sharp movements of the abdomen.
- Inhale deeply, then exhale through lips pursed but unable to whistle, but keep the air steady and smooth. The rib-cage should remain open as long as you can manage it. Let it relax gradually, as slowly as possible. If you succeeded in lasting for twenty-five seconds or more, you did well.

You should always warm up before singing. By doing as many breathing exercises as time permits you will keep your lungs in good trim.

Breathing lessons have always been high on my agenda, and I think this has paid off over the years. I remember in my first months with the Dankworth Seven some of the players, John D among them, used to visit a brass player called Phil Parker, who was in fact better known for his teaching expertise. Many non-brass players went to see him for breathing tuition, and everyone, brass students or otherwise, thought very highly of him – he had become their breathing guru.

Eager to learn and improve, I joined the disciples for a visit. Phil Parker was a no-nonsense North country man, looking as unlike a guru (whatever that might be) as one could have imagined. I'm not sure he knew what to do with a lady, especially a non-trumpet or trombone blowing lady. What I remember very vividly, after the preliminaries were over, is Mr Parker – then in his mid-seventies – lying on the floor and telling me to 'stand on this board', which he had placed across his abdomen. 'Don't be frightened, lass, you won't hurt,' he said, when he saw hesitation in my eyes. I climbed aboard and he started to inhale very slowly – a long, controlled, deep breath. I was a little worried in view of his age, but I need not have been – his stomach was as hard as a rock. With each slow breath he took I rose up in the air, and when he expelled air I came down to earth, as it were. After several ups and downs he sprang to his feet, with incredible ease for a tall, well-built man of that age, saying: 'That's the action you should always aim for, lass.'

And he didn't charge me a penny.

Section II

Train Your Ears

4

I CANNOT HOLD A TUNE

If you have been following the exercises in Section I, you should be feeling relaxed, warmed up and full of energy. The jelly roll and the musical whirl will have encouraged you to loosen up physically; pretending to be a bee and other vocal exercises will have got you used to the sound of yourself and warmed up your voice; and the breathing exercises will have given your precious lungs a good workout. As I keep stressing, singing is a physical activity, and now one of the important tools for singing well – your body – has been prepared.

But now we turn to the other important tool: your ears. In order to sing well, and in tune, you need to train these vital bits of your anatomy. In the following chapters we'll help train your ears to recognize what are called the intervals between notes, using scales and other exercises, and some simple songs you might not have sung for years.

If you have access to a piano it is, of course, an invaluable aid in helping you to discover your range (how high and low you can sing) and pitching ability. And taking up a second instrument as a hobby (if you don't play one already) can be of considerable help, not only for pitching but for many aspects of singing. An in-tune piano is a great asset when you are practising. Electronic keyboards, which can be bought in many sizes and degrees of sophistication comparatively cheaply, are a good investment, needing little or no up-keep.

I must emphasize again that one of the main things that inhibits people from singing is the belief that they cannot hold a tune. If your hearing is not impaired in any way, such as by deafness from birth or by continual abuse from loud sounds (something that is, unfortunately, becoming more prevalent in this age of high-intensity listening), what you have been given to hear with is in no way different from what is possessed by the most gifted musicians and singers in the world. Apart from the truly tone deaf, everyone can learn and improve. So let's start learning.

First of all, you must be *listening* as opposed to hearing. And you must analyse what you listen to, paying particular attention to the intervals that make up any piece.

What is an interval? Not, as far as this book is concerned, half-time at a concert, although many (musical) intervals are indeed sung at concerts! An interval is the musical distance between any two sounds. Here is a diagram explaining how this works:

Every tune consists of a series of intervals – steps of varying sizes in upward or downward directions. If you know the sound of an interval that you are required to sing you are less likely to sing it out of tune. So learning your intervals is important and the following exercises will help you to do this.

I will first show you how to sing your scale, if you don't already know how to sing one. For those with a piano or keyboard, start by finding C using the diagram overleaf.

If you don't have access to an instrument, don't worry – I will show you below how to sing a scale unaided.

Switch on your tape recorder and keep it on throughout this or any other exercise. Listen and start singing your note, slowly, gently. Then, from C, play the white keys, following the alphabet up – C D E F G A B C. This constitutes one octave, and it is the pattern of the piano from its

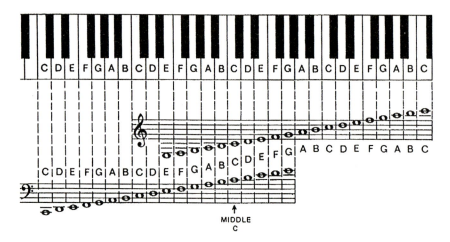

MIDDLE
C

lowest white keys all the way up to the top. Ascend slowly one note at a time, playing the next note before you sing it.

Older singers might be familiar with scales from school days, when they used to sing *doh, ray, me, fa, so, la, te, doh*. This is a music system called the tonic solfa. If you know it, it will be a great advantage to you now – recalling how you sang scales in your young days – as you go gently once again up to the top *doh*. As you sing, pay close attention to the intervals between the notes. After you have sung a scale in this way, listen carefully to yourself on your tape recorder – do your sung notes sound the same as the notes played on the piano?

For those of you without keyboard help, here is a way to sing your first scale unaccompanied. Most of you will know the carol called 'The First Nowell'. Well, whenever you sing this tune, you sing (except for two preparatory notes) a perfect scale!

With a little practice you'll soon get it. Start by singing in a low register, gently, any note you are comfortable with. Now sing 'The first Nowell the angels . . . ' Go no further than this point in the song, because from the word 'first' to the 'a' of 'angels' we have a scale. Get used to those few bars of music. Later try to think, rather than sing, the first word of the tune 'the', because it has two notes you don't need for your scale. You see, you have been singing a scale – or hearing one – for years without knowing it! To descend, sing the first four bars of 'Joy to the World'.

Here is how it looks, just to show you how clever you really are:

The— first— No - well, the— an - gels did

Joy to the world, the Lord is come.

When you can hear the scale from the word 'first', try singing it evenly, as on the lower lines – it may take a little practice, but it will be worth the effort if you are not familiar with scales.

Now that you have sung a scale, paying close attention to the intervals between notes, here is a more difficult exercise. Sit at a keyboard, play any note and then, without touching the piano, sing a scale – that is, eight ascending notes in the same pattern as before, until you reach the starting note again. (Don't forget – if you feel nervous about this – 'The First Nowell' and 'Joy to the World'.) Once you get to the same note an octave above, play that note on the piano. Is it in tune with your sung note? If not, sing the scale again, this time playing the notes on the piano, listening intently as you go. If your starting note was not a 'C', you will have noticed that you had to play some black notes to make the scale sound right. For instance, if you found your starting note was F, you would have had to play one black note (B-flat). This is because this octave is in a different key. Only the key of C uses just white notes.

To indicate the black notes in written music, we use sharps or flats. These raise or lower any note by a semitone. As you can hear, every scale has a semitone between the third and fourth notes and the seventh and eighth notes. For example, when you sang your octave from C to C, you sang semitones between E and F, and between B and the upper C (those correspond to *me* and *fa* and *te* and *doh* in tonic solfa). Sharpening or flattening a note may at first look like a problem for the beginner, but once you've learned to sing one semitone you have acquired the skill to deal with them all. A good way to practise semitones is to practise them all in sequence by using a chromatic scale, which is all semitones from beginning to end. To find any chromatic scale, pick a note on your keyboard, play it and then proceed upwards, playing the next note up, whether it happens to be a black one or a white one. The thirteenth note you play using this method will look identical to the key you started on, but it will be an octave higher. Singing along with these thirteen notes, both upwards and downwards, will give you excellent practice at singing semitones.

Now repeat the three exercises: sing a scale, playing each note before you sing it; sing a scale without the keyboard, checking your own final note against that note on the piano; and sing a chromatic scale. Try them descending as well as ascending, and listen to the results on your tape recorder. For those of you without a keyboard, sing your scale – going back to 'The First Nowell' and 'Joy to the World' if you have difficulty – and pay careful attention to the intervals between the notes. Then try singing a chromatic scale, moving up one semitone at a time.

Please don't worry if you find any of the music theory difficult. For the moment, just focus on doing the exercises to the best of your ability, really trying to listen to every note you sing and to the intervals between the notes. Use the keyboard and your tape recorder and keep practising. At this point, training your ear is more important than understanding the complexities of keys.

Remember to start comfortably low though, or you might find yourself struggling towards the end. If you find you have picked a note that is too high, stop and go lower – and if need be, lower still. Who knows – you might be a bass or baritone! Always keep in mind 'I must be comfortable'. Don't strain in either direction. Continue going up further only if you are comfortable, stopping as soon as you feel the slightest strain or discomfort.

To discover your range, choose the lowest starting note you can sing comfortably, and test how many notes you are able to go up with ease from this starting note. Ease is very important here: where you land could be the top extremity of your current vocal range. But we won't go any further into ranges here – they can always be improved with the help of a knowledgeable singing teacher.

With this little excursion up the scale, from your lowest to your highest note, you should now have a reasonable clue about the sort of songs you might eventually tackle by yourself. At this stage, if you are able to sing with ease only one octave, picking a song that has more than that is not a good idea, nor is it wise for your vocal cords. If you are having difficulty staying in tune with the keyboard (the tape recorder or a friend will tell you), difficult songs might deflate your confidence. But don't despair. You will eventually be able to sing in tune, with practice, even if you can't at the moment. All singers have to learn this. The solution is listen, practise, listen, practise – and it will come.

5

MORE ABOUT INTERVALS

Let's go back to the bees humming around the head and hum the first few bars of 'Auld Lang Syne'. Every year, all over the world this song is unthinkingly sung by people who at any other time would say 'I can't sing to save my life'. That reminds me of a comment I once heard by a father about his son: 'I know my son has a lot of music inside him, 'cos none of it has come out yet.' Oh, but it does – unknowingly – every year, and not only in Scotland on New Year's Eve. Birthdays, too, are celebrated in song, not to mention anniversaries galore, and then there are the nursery rhymes and lullabies that are sung to babies.

So let's start humming 'Auld Lang Syne' first. Easily, freely – no bawling it out as one does during the New Year festivities. This time hum it, holding on to the 'm-m' at the end of each note. Think of the song as if it were a beautiful ballad being sung to someone who is about to leave.

Hum only, following these words:
Should old acquaintance be forgot
and never brought to mind,
Should old acquaintance be forgot,
and old lang syne?

Repeat this three or four times, not singing the words for the moment, but humming softly with the buzz of the bees vibrating in your head when you reach the 'm-m' at the end of each note, all the while breathing easily. Then take a deep breath, and this time sing the words.

After the first 'forgot' take a deeper breath so you can hold the word 'mind' easily before you have to breathe for the next 'forgot', after which you take a final breath to finish with 'and old lang syne'. If you find you can sing more on one breath, don't at the moment – this exercise will help you sing slowly with ease, while sustaining your notes. Longer breaths can come later, when you are in love with the sounds you are making. Don't criticize yourself, don't be negative – just enjoy the sensation of singing this Rabbie Burns poem in a different way.

Here is the pattern to follow:

Breath . . . Should old acquaintance be forgot,
Deeper breath . . . and never brought to <u>mind</u> *(hold note)*
Deep breath . . . should old acquaintance be forgot
Breath . . . and old lang syne

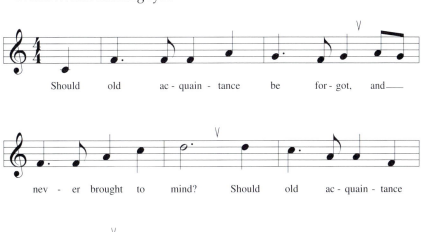

Don't forget: sing this well-known tune as a lovely slow ballad. Don't rush or push, but hold on lovingly to each word, breathing easily and listening to the sounds you are making.

When I decided to start playing the flute, the advice I was given over and over again by jazz and classical musicians alike was 'play long notes slowly, Cleo'. Long notes are good for singers to practise too – long, sustained notes. If you don't like what you hear at first, experiment with different sounds. There are so many inside you to try out. Keep going till you find one pleasing to your ear – the tape recorder can help you here.

If you find any of the exercises difficult to do, go back to where you felt at ease and start again. Keep trying until you feel satisfied with your progress, then continue. If you managed the scale and 'Auld Lang Syne', you have started to sing!

When you were singing your scale you sang the smallest intervals – tones and semitones. These are sometimes called 'seconds'. It is also vital to practise larger intervals (called 'thirds', 'fourths', 'fifths', and so on), which we will do in this chapter. In 'Auld Lang Syne' you started the song with a fourth interval, followed soon afterwards by a third.

Let's now take the song 'Three Blind Mice', learned by most five-year-olds at mum's knee, or at nursery school. If we analyse it in the same way we did 'Auld Lang Syne' you will see that mums and five-year-olds are singing thirds, fourths, a fifth and a semitone all within one octave. Let's try it:

A song sung almost daily by every generation is 'Happy Birthday', in which you have to jump one octave. Of course, if even the best singers at the celebration start the song too high, it can mean disaster of the kind I have waited for in restaurants all over the world. 'Whoops!' I think when it comes to that octave leap – but it all ends merrily.

The fact that most people can cope with these three songs shows that there is a great degree of musical know-how, sometimes unknown and wasted, in us all. If you can sing any of these songs reasonably well, then you are certainly not tone deaf, because within them are contained a lot of the basic technical needs of all singers. If you wish to sing better, work on getting these simple songs sounding good – and you are on your way.

There are many ways to remember an interval. One of the easiest for a beginner who intends to go it alone is to pick songs that you know well which start with the interval you wish to conquer, such as the ones already pointed out. 'Auld Lang Syne', for example, starts off with a fourth interval – middle C to F.

Try to discover some intervals of your own, now that you know the trick, by picking tunes out on the piano, asking a musician friend, or looking at song copies. They should come instantly to mind if they are to be really successful exercise tools, so it's better if they are tunes that have been around long enough to be sung or played *ad nauseam* and are ones you don't have to learn. You might not know the titles – you will have to find them out for your list – but as soon as you hear them you can join in with all the others, la-la-ing or humming with the best of them. Of course, each generation will have different choices, but generally you can't go wrong with celebration tunes, well-known nursery rhymes and some popular songs that have stood the test of time. So, begin to make a list from semitones, seconds, thirds, all the way up the scale. With practice, the intervals will become second nature and the songs can be discarded. This exercise is pointing out again that you know more about musical intervals than you think you do.

In the following songs the first two notes make up the interval named (unless the song is marked *, which means that the first note is repeated before the interval occurs). They are a good way to remember the 'sound' of each interval. Here is my list:

Seconds: Three Blind Mice (descending), The Man I Love, Silent
   Night
Thirds: There's No Place Like Home, Pop Goes the Weasel, Skip to

My Lou (descending), Here We Go Round the Mulberry Bush*,
The Blue Danube*

Fourths: Shenandoah, My Darling Clementine* (descending),
Auld Lang Syne, The Bluebells of Scotland, Baubles, Bangles
and Beads

Fifths: It Ain't Necessarily So, My Favourite Things, The Last Post

Sixths: My Bonnie Lies Over The Ocean, Nobody Knows the
Trouble I've Seen (descending), Speak Low, Mama's Little
Baby Loves Shortnin Bread*

Sevenths: Sorry, couldn't find any – but practise the interval

Octaves: Somewhere Over the Rainbow, Hot Cross Buns
(descending), You Go to my Head, When You Wish upon a Star,
Let it Snow

Semitones: Stardust [on the words 'Sometimes I won(der)'],
I'll Walk Alone, Oh Danny Boy

There is a diagram opposite of the first two notes of some of the songs, to
show you what they look like musically.

That's quite a few to get you started. Have fun searching for songs you
pick for yourself as well as these – it's all good training for your ears. By
the way, I had trouble finding fifths that everyone might know. You may
do better finding your very own fifth. Neither could I find a well-known
song that starts with a seventh; if you discover one please let me know.
But in any case keep practising this important interval.

Make a copy of the opening bars of your chosen songs (or mine if you
like them) to keep with you for a peek whenever you feel like testing
your skill before committing them to memory. When you feel confident
enough, look at the stave below and try to sing your intervals from
middle C – and remember to switch on your tape recorder.

Enjoy yourself! When you have memorized the intervals ascending,
start memorizing them descending. Any spare moment you have, test
your memory.

Eventually you will be able to discard your prop tunes and, when
asked, be able to sing any interval. Learning to recognize them written
on the musical stave will be a great aid in learning new songs.

If you can sing your intervals in tune – and, better still, to order when

asked to – any song is within your grasp. 'Why?' I hear you ask, 'when I learned all those songs naturally do I have to know intervals now?' Well, this knowledge will help you achieve your ambition of singing better. Lack of confidence is one of the many reasons given for not singing, and I can assure you this is a good confidence booster. You must still use your ears (in fact I would insist on it if I were your singing teacher) to learn songs. But even the best ears in the business get it wrong, and seasoned professionals often seek the help of a good rehearsal pianist to point out errant intervals. So, learning the simple basics will reinforce your confidence and prove, at least to yourself, that you are serious about singing. What I want you to do when you have managed to commit some of the intervals to your memory, is to have a daily session singing them. That will warm up your voice, exercise your ears, and help you to gain strength and flexibility – everything, in fact, you need for singing those songs which you have your ear on for the future.

6

YOU'VE GOT RHYTHM?

'The pauses between the notes – ah, that is where the art lies.'

Artur Schnabel

You should now feel more confident about carrying a tune and about recognizing the intervals between notes. But don't think you have come to the end of your singing lesson yet! You can't sing a song without knowing the rhythms that give the song its musicality and life. For the uninitiated this can be the hardest part of learning a new song; counting the bars of music is, for some, a hesitant, head-nodding, finger-counting, foot-banging nightmare. Professional singers have to know when to come in during a musical introduction. How do they do this without the conductor's obvious direction or a shove at the last minute by someone saying 'you're in'? – which is not a good idea if you want to give your all. First, they have to find out how many bars of music will be played before they start to sing, and how to count them.

First, the basics. As you've seen in earlier examples, music is written in a combination of characters and signs. The notes are written on and between five lines called a *stave* or *staff*:

The stave is divided into bars by barlines, as illustrated below:

The bars have an equal time value, and at the beginning of the music, next to the clef sign, appears the *time signature* (one number written above another), which tells you the number of notes of equal value in each bar. The top figure represents the number of beats in a bar; the figure below shows the kind of note that has one beat. If you have a piece in four/four time there will be one figure four above another, like this:

(Or possibly you may see the sign 𝄴, which is another way of indicating four/four time in printed music.)

If the piece is in three/four there will be a figure three above a figure four:

You will have to know the values of the four different kinds of notes, and also what those notes are called. Here they are:

A semibreve is a whole note, and lasts for a count of four
A minim is a half note and lasts for a count of two
A crotchet is a quarter note and lasts for one beat
A quaver is an eighth note and lasts for half a beat

Americans use the more accurate names whole, half, quarter and eighth notes, and this seems more sensible for today's student.
This is what the notes of different values look like:

Adding a dot after any of the above makes them half as long again.

Most of the songs you will want to sing will be in the easy time signatures; this means they will have two, three or four beats to a bar of music. Three/four is waltz time, two/four is generally a march. There are many others, and you might find yourself quite unknowingly singing some of the complicated ones even now – at least, they would appear complicated to you if they were written down and you were asked to sing from sight. Complication is for later if you feel you want to go further with your singing skills. For the time being, become familiar with the more common rhythms. Let us start counting bars that lead into a song with two, three or four beats to the bar. If you have the music of the song you wish to sing, take a look at the beginning of the piece to find out what the time signature is.

Because the top number is the number of beats in the bar, in four/four you would count:

1234, 2234, 3234, 4234, etc.

The first beat is always strong, the second weak, the third medium and the fourth weak. That is how you would count a four-bar musical introduction into a song. Some people find that this does not come easily, and if you think you are someone who could be a bit hesitant here, you should practise. Here are three examples you may come across:

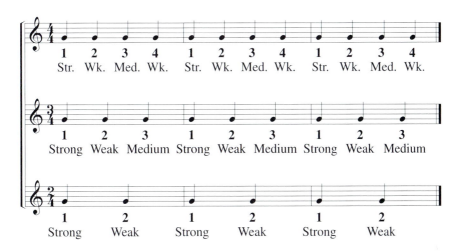

Where there is a pause or silence to be indicated in the music, this is represented by a *rest* named after the value of the note:

Semibreve rest   Minim rests   Crotchet rests   Quaver rests

To indicate the end of a piece of music a light and heavy line appear at the end of a stave:

Where part of the music should be repeated, a double bar line with two dots appears as follows:

The above is basic music theory, and understanding it will bolster your confidence. Try not to skip this or dash through it, even if you feel secure rhythmically. You will discover that practising all your new skills regularly will turn them into one strong one.

Now try using a metronome to keep in time. Set a medium tempo to begin with, and start counting over and over again. When you feel secure at that tempo, set it a little faster, until you are counting rhythmically at a reasonable speed. Do it over and over, again and again; enjoy it as a small child would on discovering the delight of being able to count up to four. A child would do it in rhythm or rhyme or dance to it. Quite a number of singers find it difficult to cope with moving and singing at the same time, so try dancing. It all helps to free tensions brought on by attempting the unknown. How about clapping, too? Whatever you choose to do, keep those ears listening to the beat of the metronome. Don't speed ahead of the beat or drag behind it, even if your one asset might be an in-born tick-tock that enables you to go in and out and across without falling into deep water, following your own drum beat while still keeping with the other's beat. The metronome is your time life-belt for now – use it to practise and eventually you will count time instinctively. When someone tells you 'I'll give you four bars in; medium tempo', your drum will click in and start working for you. It is very enjoyable. Whatever style of music you eventually want to perform, the ability to count is important in enabling you to keep together with the musicians, or to come in or drop out when the written music says so.

When you feel happy with 4/4, go on to 3/4 then 2/4. Don't move on until you are able to count freely and naturally. The way 3/4 is counted has a definite sound and rhythm. One is always the strong beat, two and three are weak. If you have ever had to learn how to waltz you will be streets ahead here. And marching in 2/4 to a Sousa march is strong/weak, strong/weak, strong/weak.

When you were a child did you ever play the game of 'Guess the Tune' by clapping out the rhythms of a tune? When we had a family game, I always found it difficult to guess the song if there were too many pauses with a count of four or more beats. The more notes in the bar, the merrier for me. The songs had to be popular ditties, or at least known to the family, otherwise you would get into trouble with your opponents and they would think up something obscure to take revenge on you. If you deviated by adding notes and not giving full values, but the song was eventually guessed, siblings would give you a hard time. So it was always best not to cheat but to stick to the rules. This game kept me and my brother and sister amused when we were young, while at the same time teaching us the rhythms of songs. Later, my own children enjoyed playing on long car journeys and holidays. It's an excellent start to sight-reading new songs, since once you have understood the rhythms, by clapping the values of notes and the patterns that often repeat in a song, you are halfway there. It is amazing how tunes jump into your head when you are hand-clapping rhythms, and also how the originality and uniqueness of individual songs are made more apparent. When you understand the values of notes and pauses in the structure of a song, it is easy to clap your way through any written music and make tunes you know by ear a fun game. You are also allowed to la, la-dee dee-du or ta on one note – never give away any of the other notes. Both ways are valuable exercises and will help strengthen your rhythmical ability and therefore your confidence.

As an exercise, try clapping out the rhythms of the songs on pages 71 to 80. The songs are all well known, but seeing them written out as music will make you concentrate on and think about the rhythms a little more deeply.

Many of the students who were at the Wavendon course had weaknesses in the rhythm department – they had bar-counting problems, and would come in too early when a note had to be held, or in a bar of music that had a rest of any kind. This is not unusual – it happens to the best of us, and not only singers. I introduced the clapping game to the class, and we all had some fun guessing songs, some of which were certainly unknown to me. Building up one's ability and confidence means practice. Practice – to be able to stand without singing while the music is being played and not feel like a beached whale. Confidence – to count silently, silently the length of a rest in music before coming in again with complete assurance to sing the next note. Listening, counting, listening, counting; listening to recordings of accomplished singers singing all kinds of music is always a good idea too. Eventually your own style will break through.

I have in my repertoire a parody of a young girl who is taking part in a talent competition. On occasion I have performed it for a bit of fun at the tutors' concerts that are put on for students and public at the end of a course. It is a bit of fun, but it is also a lesson – a lesson in choice and preparation, pointing out how an important appearance can be ruined by the wrong material and, even more important if you are serious, by not doing your homework. This young lady has chosen to sing a song that is highly sophisticated and that does not suit her dramatic or musical abilities. She is naïve and quite artless. The song needs a degree of experience to put it across, and it does not sit well on her young shoulders on any count. Before I go into the caricature I sing the song straight – that is, the telling of the story of 'The Lorelei' by Ira and George Gershwin. The audience is unaware at this stage that it is going to develop into comedy.

At the end of the 'serious' performance the band plays a vamp (a section of the music played continuously over and over again for a performer to make an announcement, dance or perform magic), and this gives me time to explain to the audience the young girl's misjudgement in picking this particular song and how it went awfully wrong for her.

The serious 'Lorelei'

I then slip into her character, portraying the timing and rhythms that are a mess, although she is blissfully unaware of this as she ploughs on, crossing and dropping beats. She counts audibly under her breath, which is painfully obvious to the audience and annoying for the musicians, who have realized after a couple of bars that they are now trying to catch up and stay with her and the beats that she liberally drops and adds in each bar. Still quite oblivious of the panic she is creating behind her, she carries on, happily enjoying being stage-struck. At this point, and as one, the musicians start listening intently, realizing that the song could come to a standstill, with everything and everyone collapsing into an embarrassing, messy end if they do not follow this untutored, ingenuous creature who is in it over her head. They (just about) save her day, and although she is quite ignorant of this, the audience is not.

It is a cruel but entertaining portrayal of a lot of singers I have heard over the years (indeed, I was once one of them), and it does amuse the audience, as they gradually realize that they have sat through this for real a few times. The students always see the funny side of it, as they have had over a week of intensive tuition, correcting and pointing out their pitfalls. But they also know they will go home with a lot more knowledge than the young girl I presented to them. And so will you if you practise the exercises in this chapter.

Section III

Practice Makes Perfect

7

INTERPRETATION

Perfect tuning and perfect timing are important, but they are not all that's necessary to sing a song well. To sing beautifully you must also be aware of phrasing and meaningful interpretation. In this chapter we look at how you should approach any song you want to learn, and study in more detail a song that my students at Wavendon have found useful, and one possible way of interpreting it.

If you have chosen a piece through hearing a recording of it, do your utmost to acquire a copy of the sheet music. It is important to know the original and correct tune and lyrics from the outset. Many renditions on records are improvisations based on the original tune, and if you sing them that way, you are telling the world you are a copycat!

Whenever you sing, pick a simple ditty that is well within your vocal capabilities. Don't pick an operatic aria or a heavy rock number if you're short of range for opera or if your voice is too sweet and gentle for heavy rock. There are innumerable kinds of song, written and designed for every conceivable type of voice and vocal ability. Spend time in searching out the right one for yourself.

After you have memorized the correct tune, commit the lyrics to memory as soon as possible, because uncertainty makes you sing inwardly, and without conviction. Study the lyrics for their poetry, and be aware of any rhyming schemes the lyricist has worked hard to produce. Understand the story being told within the song – if you don't comprehend it yourself your audience will not believe you. If there are any difficult bars or intervals that you keep getting wrong, find a friend who plays the piano (if you don't play yourself) who would be willing to go over these spots again and again with you. Or, even if you are only capable of playing one-finger piano, set about doing this for yourself.

Memorizing gets easier the more you have to do it, so memorize something new every week – if not a song try a poem.

Always look closely at an unfamiliar piece of music to discover if there is a pattern that you know and, if you do, how many times it will be repeated. These discoveries are a bonus in learning time, as the unfamiliar can then command all your attention and concentration during practice sessions. You can use your interval song guide or the piano to work on any difficult and unfamiliar musical patterns. You will also discover that you know more than you give yourself credit for – a good fillip for your confidence.

Wavendon students concentrating

Now study the lyrics and the music that follow. This is a song that was written specially for the Wavendon course, for reasons I'll explain later. Try to find the right key for your voice, and then try to learn the song. If this is too advanced for you, find someone with keyboard skills to help you.

To find out if a key is acceptable for your voice, find the highest and lowest notes in the song on the piano or pitch pipe. If you can sing both notes with ease, then in all probability the written key you have chosen will be suitable. If you wish to take the song up or down in pitch, sing the song in your most comfortable range, and the note on which you finish will be the key. For safety's sake, tell the pianist your starting note too.

How Birds Can Sing

music copyright © John Dankworth
lyrics copyright © Cleo Laine

How many ways do you think you could interpret the song, without making a mockery of the sentiments it intended to express? Read the lyrics, and think about any particular feeling they arouse in you. Do they make you think about sadness or joy? Do they make you feel melancholy or optimistic? If you have no strong reaction, use your imagination and make one up. If you feel a mixture of emotions, this is fine too – the mixing of feelings can bring light and shade to an interpretation.

The next stage is to introduce dynamics, which provide further light and shade at certain obvious points within the song, so that it is not sung all on one level. Singing on one level can be effective with certain voices and styles of songs, but in this song there are moments that need to be brought out with extra intensity, which means more breath and control. This will also lead to better pitching of some of the intervals.

In fact, there is a hidden pitching exercise in the song that will be beneficial – it was specially composed this way to help the Wavendon students. If you look at the first six bars of the tune without paying attention to the time values of the notes, you should see that it is a succession

Students throwing themselves into a song

of ever-widening intervals, starting with a second, then a third, then a fourth and so on, the top notes of which form the pattern of an ascending scale, going from D to B above. Each upper note goes back down to C every time, before hitting the next interval up the scale. The composer has made a song out of a well-known pitching exercise for singers and instrumentalists, an exercise that should or could be done daily to improve one's ear. So interval practice comes into play immediately in the song, eventually arriving at the octave (bar 27). Later there is an option to sing the lower C (bar 29).

Most songs are based on the notes in the major scale, whatever key they may be in. Some, indeed, use the major scale itself as the basis of their construction. 'The First Nowell', for example, uses (after two introductory notes) an ascending major scale. 'Joy to the World' takes the opposite course and utilizes a descending major scale for its first bars. All songs, however simple or otherwise, are constructed from scales and intervals – the patterns are limitless – so if you practise both frequently you will recognize them when they turn up.

Phrasing is one of the important aspects of singing a song and can, of course, be tackled in different ways depending on the style of the singer. A relaxed delivery with a sincere reading of the words should be your main aim. I'll take you through the song with one possible interpretation, just to show you how it can be done.

Try to sing the first four bars of our song on one breath, in a reflective, tranquil mood, sung at a medium volume. Then, taking a good deep breath, go for the first heightening of expression. For the next four bars, the breath should be controlled, to support the higher notes that you are about to sing, moderately loud on the words 'wake' and 'morning', going for a bright sound, without too much emphasis on the words (a little common sense here will prevent you from over-doing things, which could sound corny). Come down to *sotto voce*, which means a low voice, and almost a conversational quality, on the words 'Yet I don't hear them', to build yet again towards and to linger a little on the phrase 'prepare their song'. The word 'song' should be given its full value and sung meaningfully. Make the most of 'I'd like their secret, to sing along'.

The next section should start with a lighter, brighter feel. It can be broken up after 'sunshine' with a small breath, to continue with 'and skies of blue'. Then try a long phrase. So take a deep breath and go for

'They've found the freedom of singing true', and another big breath to support a strong finish. There could even be a slight slowing down (*ritenuto,* or *rit*) on the words 'I'll keep on seeking that special thing'. If you hit the top note at this point, don't do it a second time, go to the lower note at the end of the song, or vice versa. If you intend finishing with the different lyrics after singing the 32-bar chorus, you must go back to the bar before letter D in the music, to sing the first three notes of the lyrics, which are: 'They send a'. Another possible ending is to go back to a bar before C, carry on until you get to the bar before D, then change to the new lyrics. Whatever you decide to do, definitely finish the first chorus on the lower note, so that you can give your all to the reprise of the last eight bars for your 'big' ending.

This is a guide only, and the suggestions for interpretation will not suit everybody. If my way doesn't work for you, experiment. Find a way that suits your style and that makes musical sense for you. If it is not possible for you to control your breath for any reason, it should still be easy to make sense of the words and convey their meaning by singing two bars at a time, even interrupting a sentence with a breath after two words, such as after the long held note on the word 'sing' (breathe), 'I wake' (breathe) 'each morning', so that the high note B of 'morning', that has to be pitched from the word 'each' on middle C (a 7th interval) stands a chance of being in tune. Try what seems to you to be the hard way first, then adjust things if you find you are straining or running out of breath.

I have given here only one possible interpretation of one song, but it shows you some of the things you should be aware of when you are learning and thinking about how to sing a piece in the most meaningful way. Varying the dynamics, phrasing, colour and mood of a song will make it more musical and more interesting for the listener.

But an interpretation should never be contrived – it should always express what the song makes you feel; and although forethought and preparation are vital, when it comes to performance you should be as spontaneous as possible. In the end, the important thing is to try to sing any song as naturally as you can.

8

SOUND

The sounds that emanate from the throats of singers are numerous, and each individual performer might be described by a devotee in rhapsodic terms that to non-fans seem undeserved. Those sounds can range from gloriously pure to roughened by whisky and cigarettes, with every perceivable sound in between. Sound will always be a matter of taste, no matter what style of music one sings.

What one pair of ears or set of senses finds great delight in, another will find infuriating. The wide differences of sound made by internationally known singers encompass the full range that the instrument called 'voice' is capable of producing, from the worlds of opera, jazz, folk, rock, pop and show tune singing. If, therefore, when you listened to your voice for the first time on tape you thought it awful, or you have been told over and over again to shut up because someone else thinks it's awful and you are convinced that it cannot be altered to sound better, I would ask you to think or try again, because the quality or tone of a voice can always be improved.

People in the public eye have been going to specialists for years. Politicians and actors, lecturers, TV personalities – all of them go to vocal coaches to cultivate a softer, more mature tone if they feel they come across as too rasping, hard-edged or nasal. A singer can do the same. The emotions that are expressed in speech – anger, love, joy, fear, confidence – can alter the sound of your voice instantaneously. When you're angry, your voice becomes louder, harder edged. If you're in love and talking to the person of your dreams in an intimate mood, you modulate your voice and achieve gentle tones; and you would find a soothing sound to calm a crying baby, and another soothing, but different sound to reassure someone who was elderly. Think for a moment how most people change their sound when they talk to a hard-of-hearing person or a foreigner – the change can be quite dramatic. You can recall these emotions to your advantage if you want to change your speaking voice, as exceptional actors have shown. Even if you are not experiencing these feelings in reality, using your imagination can have powerful effects.

Transferred from the speaking to the singing voice, imagination can work wonders. When you sing any song for the first time, or even one you may have lived with for years, experiment. Different tone colours will come about if you recall as many of the emotions you have experienced as you possibly can. If you are unable to do this, place yourself in another person's situation. Put circumstances and feelings in your head and they will, with practice, come out of your mouth – through volume changes, singing higher or lower, producing more energy or intensity. Listen, listen, listen, always, for that change that might be right for you. Remember what brought it about and use it until it becomes second nature. Words, and how they are used, can also alter the quality of sound. If you make the most of your consonants by exaggerating them, and sing shorter vowels, you will get a percussive, marching feel. Switching to sustained vowels will bring about a more intense rendition. 'Auld Lang Syne' is a great song to work with. Try to find as many different ways of singing it as you can, to discover sounds you think don't exist within you. Experiment.

Clear articulation is important, and can have quite an effect on a song. Here are some exercises to help you practise the different sounds of vowels and consonants.

Vowels
To practise vowel sounds, do the following:

Say ee, ah, oo.
Now *whisper* each sound three times.
Speak each sound three times.
Again *whisper* each sound three times.

Now, using the example below
Sing the pattern three times, with one vowel and one breath.

SING ee _
SING ah _
SING oo _

Repeat the exercise using different pitches and volumes.

When you are whispering, watch yourself in the mirror, and note the position of your lips, tongue and jaw. Tape record the whispered and sung vowels to help you decide if they sound clear and distinct and resonant.

Consonants

Consonants are sounds produced when the vocal air flow is interrupted by lips, teeth or tongue. Because of the way they are produced, consonants, unlike vowels, have poor carrying power. The clear articulation of consonants is, therefore, of great importance in conveying the required sound to the listener, both in speech and singing.

The English language contains twenty-five consonant sounds. Once a singer has learned how each of these is produced and articulated, he or she must practise them all at length. Only by means of such practice will a singer achieve vital sound clarity and learn how to make the most of varying emphasis, energy, style, mood and emotion when performing.

Listening to the different sounds that professional singers make can inform you about the sound that you are after better than anything that might be written down. Hearing something that you would like to express yourself helps you to get to the nub of things quickly. Inevitably, there are certain physical boundaries that will always determine the colour of our voices. These boundaries are, in the main, obvious: sex, and the shape of the head and body. Then there is what is called tessitura: the four or five notes that can be sung most easily by a singer. There is range; there is also how much natural power one has. All of these factors determine whether you are a natural soprano, mezzo, contralto, tenor, baritone, or bass.

Here is a diagram showing the approximate ranges of each category of voice:

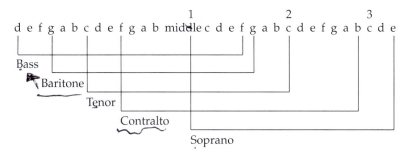

In addition, there is resonance; we resonate every time we speak or sing, and with practice we can achieve more or less resonance, as well as volume and tone, by changing the shape or position of our lips, tongue, jaw, soft palate and larynx.

Here are some exercises that should be done regularly to help improve tone, range and power.

Sigh on the vowel 'ah', starting on the highest comfortable note, softly sighing down to the lowest comfortable note, and doing this several times, which is also an exercise that helps to blend uneven registers. After doing several soft sighs, switch to a series of broken ones; then go back to long sighs, starting softly, finishing louder, still 'ah-ing' from top to bottom.

Women   Men

Sighing exercises

Now do some 'yawn sighs' (not a full yawn, just the start – don't finish it, because it's hard to stop a full yawn once started; it becomes very catching and you get a whole class of yawners). It is a key exercise, as it produces an open throat, a desirable position for singing. So take a breath, begin but don't finish a yawn, sigh on 'ah' once again, on a comfortable note, descending to the lowest, observing the sensation in the throat and the position of the larynx, which should be low, but not depressed. (The larynx, for those who don't know, is the bump in the throat under the chin, more prominent in men than most women.) The tip of the tongue should lie naturally and comfortably at the base of the bottom front teeth. Once again, repeat this exercise several times, alternating medium loud and loud volumes, always at comfortable pitches.

Some singers have difficulty with singing softly, and find that they can sing properly only when they are singing out. If you want to sing a lullaby or gentle ballad, how can you improve your soft voice? It is not easy, if you have always sung full tilt, to switch to a soft style – it will take intelligent concentration and practice. Using imagery when you are singing can help. Try thinking 'lullaby', no matter what type of song you may be singing; or that you are serenading a shy or frightened person.

Singing 'I am a Woman', with Caterina Valenti and Petula Clark

Alternatively, try taking a good deep breath, and start a loud note, singing 'ah'; then gradually, and with control, change to 'oo', all the while making it quieter, softer, quieter, softer, almost to nothing. Then slowly (take your time) broaden out again, to a loud note on 'ah'. Do it very slowly. Keep within your range without any strain. If you feel any stress whatever, stop; relax, breathe, and keep in mind that although the 'ah' is open, it is not down in the throat – that way lies trouble. Have a yawn, wide, and notice how your throat feels – open and wide – and remember that all the time when you are singing. Keep it up, high in front of the head, just below the nose (not in it) or above the top teeth. Each time you perform this exercise, try to remember the sensations you felt as you went from *forte* (loud) to *sotto voce* (soft), and vice versa.

I have listed below a selection of singers, who come from different musical disciplines, all with individual sounds of their own, to illustrate the vast range of sounds the human voice is capable of producing, sometimes from one person. They are not in any order of preference, and certainly not the last word in selection. They may all be very different from one another, but they all have style – love it or hate it.

'There is no beauty without strangeness in the proportions.'

Christopher Marlowe

Classical

Marian Anderson	Janet Baker	Enrico Caruso
Maria Callas	Dietrich Fischer-Dieskau	Lesley Garrett
Marilyn Horne	Anna Moffo	Birgit Nilsson
Luciano Pavarotti	Joan Sutherland	Sarah Walker
Placido Domingo	Beniamino Gigli	Peter Pears
Geraint Evans	Joan Hammond	Richard Tauber
José Carreras	Ben Luxon	Nicolai Gedda
Robert Tear	Kiri Te Kanawa	Beverly Sills
Montserrat Caballé	Teresa Berganza	Kirsten Flagstad
Elisabeth Schwarzkopf	Rosa Ponselle	Lottie Lehmann

Jazz/Soul

Louis Armstrong	Tony Bennett	Ray Charles
Bing Crosby	Blossom Dearie	Billy Eckstein
Ella Fitzgerald	Billie Holiday	Al Jarreau
Peggy Lee	Carmen McRae	Anita O'Day
Annie Ross	Bessie Smith	Jack Teagarden
Mel Tormé	Sarah Vaughan	Fats Waller
Joe Williams	Frank Holder	Jimmy Rushing
Jon Hendricks	Aretha Franklin	Dee Dee Bridgewater
Nat King Cole	Patti Austin	Mark Murphy
Norma Winstone	Nancy Wilson	Nina Simone
Diana Reeves	Bette Carter	

Standard/Show tunes

Fred Astaire
Noël Coward
Lena Horne
Anthony Newley
Whitney Houston
Petula Clark
Liza Minnelli
Julie Andrews
Vera Lynn

Shirley Bassey
Sammy Davis Jr
Peggy Lee
Frank Sinatra
Betty Buckley
Caterina Valenti
Bette Midler
Edith Piaf
Nelson Eddy

Bing Crosby
Judy Garland
Johnny Mathis
Barbra Streisand
Bernadette Peters
Chita Rivera
Ethel Merman
Diana Ross

Folk/Rock

Joan Armatrading
Kiki Dee
Janis Joplin
Rod McEwan
Roy Orbison
Dionne Warwick
Hank Williams
James Taylor
Bonnie Tyler
Sam Cooke

Joan Baez
Georgie Fame
John Lennon
Randy Newman
Patti Page
Paul McCartney
David Bowie
Tina Turner
Harry Belafonte
Carole King

Cher
Billy Joel
Joni Mitchell
Laura Nyro
Stevie Wonder
Elvis Presley
Bruce Springsteen
k.d. lang
Rod Stewart
Elton John

9

ESTABLISH A ROUTINE

Have a little break from studying at this point. Now is the time (having kept to a regular practice schedule) to review how you are doing. If you have kept a record of your work so far on your tape recorder (if not you must start to) go right back to your first renditions, listen attentively with your new listening ears, then whiz forward to the last lesson you gave yourself. Well? Did you hear a difference? Any difference in your breath control, ease of execution, pitching, sound, strength, rhythm, or a different feel in anything, anywhere? If you are unable to be objective about your work, let a good friend, or a complete stranger, have a listen to the two tracks, one after the other. Don't explain anything, just ask 'What do you think about these two recordings of mine?' Then sit back and wait with your fingers crossed for their verdict. But don't get upset if they say they like the first one better. It is quite possible at this stage – effort and concentration on individual points could make you sound precise and unnatural. Don't worry! The time will come when you will stop thinking about doing the right things in the right place, and then you will sound and feel at ease, comfortable and unstrained. You will sound as natural as a bird.

Decide for yourself what you need to improve. You have the basic information now to do that. If you want to go further, find a good singing teacher. Or just enjoy the new-found knowledge that you can now hold a tune.

You know, the more you sing the better you will get at doing it. I'm not telling you anything new or profound. Maxims abound, and are constantly repeated, on the drawbacks or benefits of keeping on top of anything one may be studying, such as 'practice makes perfect', 'use it or lose it', 'however much thou art read in theory, if thou hast no practice thou art ignorant' and so on. So if you keep up your practice you will not get bombarded with all those 'mumsie' homilies.

Imagine yourself to be a world-class athlete getting ready to appear at the next Olympic Games. Hold that image in your mind. Now imagine you are a prima ballerina preparing for a premier performance of *Swan Lake* at a renowned venue, or a solo musician about to appear at an important concert. Maybe you are a champion heavy-weight boxer about to defend his title, or an international ice skater, or ballroom dancer, or tennis player. You've got the picture? Now, what would all these wonderful people be doing daily? Well, hopefully, they would be preparing for the daunting tasks they will have to face by themselves. That would mean getting their muscles toned, strengthened and honed to withstand all that the body and mind must endure on the day of performance. It will be quite an exhausting regime for each one of them, and it will not depend on their position or status in the league of their chosen profession. It is a requirement for all, without any question.

And so it goes for the aspiring singer at any level. It is common sense that a muscle works better when it is gently warmed up. So much benefit can be gained by warming up vocal cords daily. Whether you intend to sing or not, the exercises will be strengthening and relaxing, enabling you to tackle songs with much more skill and assurance. So I do recommend that you take a look at the suggested routines and try to fit in a warm-up every day. A short one is better than none at all. If, of course, you are going to perform, you should always warm up the vocal cords and get rid of any tension you might have anywhere in the body, especially the neck and shoulders.

Our objectives have been to help you relax, control your breathing, and listen to your pitching and sound. Go over everything you have learned so far, trying to stick to it on a regular basis. The more you do, the faster your progress will be, even if you do only a small amount each time. Perhaps there is something standing out on your tape that you are not sure you like, but you are unable to put your finger on exactly what it is. Try to work out what is bothering you, by seeing if it is lurking in the list below and by listening again and again. If you think you have found the cause of your discontent, spend a little more time doing the appropriate exercise to improve what displeases you. But please – I cannot emphasize this enough – never, ever, tire or strain yourself aiming for perfection. Does it exist?

First, here is a list of problem spots for you to listen out for on your tape, together with the exercises that could put them to rights.

Pitching

- Play, listen, sing the note.
- Practise your song intervals, up and down, checking with piano keyboard or pitch pipe.
- Sing and record well-known nursery rhymes.
- Record and listen, record and listen to everything.

Breathing

- Concentrate on listening to your breathing when you are doing any exercise, especially breathing exercises.
- Mark where you are going to breathe when you practise a song.
- Do not try to do too much on one breath – running out of breath can affect the pitch.

Breath control

- Sing long held notes on all the vowels, softly and loudly.
- Take a breath counting four – hold for four – let out for a count of four. Slowly work up to a count of eight if you are comfortable, and there is no tension.

Perceived sound – too loud, soft, harsh, nasal, throaty, and so on

- Sing and record the same song several times, each time thinking of different emotions or situations, such as love, anger, passion, tenderness (to child, mother, father and so on), lullabies, hymns, joy, childlike, boy, girl, etc.
- Use your imagination. If, when you listen again, one sound pleases you more than another, try to recall the emotion that brought it about and sing with this feeling uppermost in your heart when you practise anything for a while.
- Record again after a few sessions of doing this, then listen to the results; if you feel your sound has improved from your first perceived sound, then keep up the practice – you will gain a sound you like better – and a bargain-price acting lesson.

When you do sing naturally about the house, or at any time, don't get worried if these exercises don't fall into place – forget about them: just sing. It's the daily practice that you put in that will make it all fall into place quite naturally. Even some professional singers concentrate too much on technique while they are performing so that it affects their performance – for example, they worry about their breathing, when they should just let it come naturally, or they are so busy worrying about whether their tongues are placed correctly that they can't give the music the inspiration and expression it needs.

Finally, here is a routine incorporating some of these exercises for you to follow when you have a period set aside for yourself:

- Always, always start with the breathing exercises. This is important not only for your singing health but also for your body's well-being. One cannot function well if the other is out of sorts. Breathing exercises are also the prime means of relaxing all the major muscle groups of the body, the destroyer of nerves and performance jitters.
- When you feel comfortable, do three or four jelly rolls. Bend over from the hips and hang (don't force anything; if you are unable to hang, go as far as you comfortably can – a little a day will soon get you over). Then gently roll back up, knees bent, one vertebra at a time.
- If you are in the least bit tense, open your mouth wide and yawn. Then, with your mouth still open, allow the weight of your head to take the ear to each shoulder (don't let your shoulders ride up – keep them relaxed and down), first left then right. Keep yawning. A slow count of five each side is enough. Don't bounce and don't force anything. You can do this at any time of the day if you feel the need.
- If your energy level is low, or you need to wake yourself up, have a dance to some bright music that you enjoy.
- Now get down to some bee humming, going through all the vowel sounds: A, E, I, O, U.
- With your tape recorder on, concentrate on long, slow, smooth notes, in an easy register – listening, concentrating, listening, listening.
- From there, work on the intervals you have learned, or try to learn

one. Start with the smallest interval first, up and down, then work towards the widest you have grasped so far. If you have memorized any, keep them fresh and add another.

• Finish with more breathing.

Here is the circle of exercises, your daily life giver:

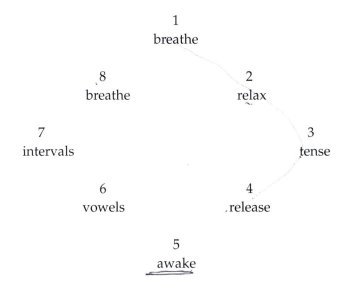

1
breathe

8   2
breathe   relax

7   3
intervals   tense

6   4
vowels   release

5
awake

Do this regularly and the old chestnut joke could well apply to you – 'How do you get to Carnegie Hall? Practise my friend, practise.'

Section IV

Songs to Practise On

I include here some simple songs, all of which have just an octave range, for you to practise your new skills on. They are songs you probably know, but you might not have seen them as written music before now. Use them to practise in a variety of ways. First, clap the rhythms. Then see if you can spot the intervals in the pieces and sing them. Now practise your vowels and consonants – sing the songs with clipped sounds, like a march; then sing them with elongated vowels, like a lullaby. Keep referring back to earlier chapters if you get stuck.

You should tape yourself singing them, using a variety of sounds and styles. Use them to experiment with – and have fun!

Michael, Row the Boat Ashore

This Old Man

1. This   Old   Man,   he   played   one,   He   played   knick - knack

on   my___ thumb, with   a   knick - knack   pad - dy whack,   give   a   dog   a   bone,

This   Old   Man came   roll - ing   home.   2. This   Old   Man,   he   played   two,

He   played knick - knack   on   my___ shoe, with   a   knick - knack   pad - dy whack

give   a   dog   a   bone,   This   Old   Man   came   roll - ing   home.

3. This Old Man, he played three,
He played knick-knack on my knee,
With a knick-knack paddy whack, give a dog a bone,
This Old Man came rolling home.

4. This Old Man, he played four,
He played knick-knack on my door,
With a knick-knack paddy whack, give a dog a bone,
This Old Man came rolling home.

5. This Old Man, he played five,
He played knick-knack on my hive,
With a knick-knack paddy whack, give a dog a bone,
This Old Man came rolling home.

6. This Old Man, he played six,
He played knick-knack on my sticks,
With a knick-knack paddy whack, give a dog a bone,
This Old Man came rolling home.

When the Saints Go Marching In

Amazing Grace

Tit Willow

Nobody Knows the Trouble I've Seen

No - bod - y knows the trou- ble I've seen, No - bod - y knows such

sor - row, No - bod - y knows the trou- bles I've seen,

Glo - ry Hal - le - lu - jah! Some - times I'm up, some -

times I'm down;———— Oh, yes, Lord! Some -

times I'm al- most to the ground,———— Oh, my,— Lord!

Old MacDonald

2. Cat   Meow Meow   5. Hoe   Hoe Hoe
3. Sheep   Baa Baa   7. Horse   Neigh Neigh
4. Cow   Moo Moo   8. Shovel   Dig Dig

Bluebells of Scotland

Bobby Shaftoe

Cockles and Mussels

Section V

The Pleasures and Pitfalls of Performing

10

SHOWING OFF YOUR NEW-FOUND SKILLS

One of the best ways to practise and enjoy singing is in the company of other like-minded people. This will mean a little detective work on your part, finding the best way to proceed to achieve your goals. One obvious way is to join a choir or group that takes beginners. Not only do you get the opportunity to sing regularly with others, but, where mixed groups are concerned, you will be with other beginners as well as with experienced singers who will show you the ropes. Enquire, too, about the many groups that consist of complete beginners, who sing just for the fun of it rather than for performance. Choirs that tackle harmonically intricate music generally require good sight-reading skills, but there is no harm in asking. Do investigate your local church choirs, women's organizations, music groups, barber's shop choirs, male voice choirs, or children's music groups, to find out their requirements. There will be a list of the choirs in your area in your local library or music college – they vary widely from small chamber choirs to enormous choirs with hundreds of members, and with every permutation between. There is often a great need for participants, and membership of such groups can lead to enjoyable musical and social experiences. The choir master is usually experienced not only in musical direction but often in vocal training as well, so an added benefit is care and further training of the voice when you are rehearsing and performing. You could take up a singing course at your local college – these are often taught in groups, and will give you a chance to sing solo in front of other people in a supportive environment. You could also try a summer school – or come to Wavendon!

A choir at Wavendon – me in the left hand corner directing their efforts
(my hair gives me away)

If you like folk music, folk sessions in pubs can provide a welcoming environment in which to try out your vocal skills – singing either with others, or as a soloist. And there are pubs and jazz clubs with open-mike policies, where you can try out singing before an audience.

If all you want, now that you have at last found a singing voice, is to let fly freely and comfortably, when you feel like it and for your own enjoyment, that is wonderful too, as long as you don't neglect to do it. If you have friends who love to sing, suggest getting together for a regular weekly sing-song instead of your other pursuits. Holiday courses are another possibility; the companionship of other people who feel the way you do is one of the main attractions of weekend and short-stay music courses. You can learn a great deal at these courses, whether you are a novice or an experienced performer, and if you have ambitions to become a soloist, they are a way of making contact with good tutors, who could guide you in the search for a teacher who would be right for your particular needs.

Then there is always the ubiquitous karaoke – for many it can be a fun way of satisfying an urge to perform. It can also provide an opportunity to get some microphone practice. On the few occasions when I have been in a place where it has been in operation, the performers have certainly needed lessons in microphone technique. If you are one of the many, when you get the chance, do turn it into a practice session as well as a bit of fun. Handle and use the microphone gently and with class. Please! don't bang it or blow into it before you start to see if it's on – it will be! Other things to be avoided are bawling into it, sticking it up your nose, and clutching it for dear life. Try a little subtlety. The microphones in these situations are not state of the art, so see if you can at least make the equipment seem better than it really is. (See Chapter 11 for more on this important aspect of performing.)

Wherever you are singing, at whatever level, always warm up – if you were an athlete you would not think of going to run, jump, kick or swim without first warming up your muscles, for fear of injury. The same applies for a singer who is going to perform. Start off with gentle long notes that are well within your range. Then, if what you have to sing has difficult passages, go over these tricky parts, carefully picking out unusual intervals, passages in the extremities of your range, tongue-twisting words, phrases with breathing problems and so on. Have a tape made of your necessary exercises, played by a friend, teacher or your-self. With this to hand you will not have to rely on anyone for your warm-up, and you won't need to be near a piano or have the inconvenience of not being able to get to one.

Nerves often arise if you are unsure of what you are doing, so do your homework about the songs you want to sing. If you are still nervous, no matter how well prepared you are, breathing exercises do help – long, slow breaths to calm you down. And why not try telling yourself: 'The audience can't do what I'm about to, so why should they scare me?'

I have worked with some singers (indeed, some very famous ones) who need anxiety, and have to create it themselves to be able to perform. Other singers need to meditate. And then there are the majority who just get on and do it. They love to sing, and nothing's going to take away the enjoyment they derive from it. The old adage that says 'all the best performers suffer nerves' is nonsense. Implying that fear is necessary to perform well is merely an anodyne, employed to calm some artistes down. You either have nerves or you don't. If you do, you overcome them. If you can't overcome your nerves and they continue to affect your performance badly, no matter what you do to stop them, perhaps it might be best to look into another side of the profession. Singing should make you feel alive and happy, not miserable with fear!

If you decide to go further than choirs and karaoke, you may find yourself at a venue where there are live musicians who might accompany you, either a solo pianist, or a rhythm section – bass, drums, piano. Do find out what the policy of the bar is before you approach the musicians. Sometimes it is publicized outside that talent is welcome or you may hear about it on the grapevine. If not, ask the bar staff whether they welcome singers or other musicians sitting in. If they do, please be prepared when you get up to perform. Know what you intend to sing – the key, the tempo and how many bars intro you want. Seek the help of a musician friend if all or some of this is a little out of your reach at the moment. Perform songs that you know well and stick to them until you have built up a repertoire, when you can switch quickly if necessary. Keep a book with keys, titles and information about the songs, such as the names of the composer and lyricist and when it was composed. Audiences like to know – as do the musicians who will accompany you. Don't pick obscure pieces that they are unlikely to know. For instance, if the group or pianist has played standards all night, it would be wise to choose a standard to sing; a current favourite pop song of yours may be asking for trouble – and vice versa, if you were to ask a rock, pop or folk oriented band to play standard tunes. So listen, and choose your material sensibly for those occasions when you feel like taking the plunge into the pub world.

If you know what you want from your arrangements with bands and you are qualified to explain, there should not be any problem – if you are a tactful person. If, on the other hand, you are neither tactful nor qualified, you have a big problem. So the best way to deal with it is as follows:

- Always find out who the leader of the group is and introduce yourself.
- Own up if your knowledge is limited.
- Always treat musicians with respect, and they will usually reciprocate.

Good luck with whatever musical avenue you pursue!

11

THE ALCHEMY OF ACOUSTICS AND AMPLIFICATION

Amplification and the art of using a microphone may well eventually become part of your vocal technique – your 'instrument', in fact – and they should be studied if you intend to use them. They can enhance low, soft notes that you would never attempt without their aid, allowing them to be heard at the back of a large concert hall or above accompaniment that might be going at full tilt, something that happens in some of today's music. The decision whether to use a microphone or not will depend on the kind of music you perform, where that performance will take place and the backing or instrumentation that is played behind you.

When you take all these considerations into account, as well as the type of song, there is quite a lot to learn. First and foremost you need to be heard by everyone present, but without blasting the front rows out of their seats in an effort to reach the back of the hall. In some places this is not easy to accomplish, but with the advances in all aspects of sound engineering, most important new halls being built today have systems installed that overcome this problem. Modern, state-of-the-art sound systems in these places allow for an equal overall sound to be heard anywhere in the auditorium at a level that is comfortable for the listener. Wherever you are singing, it is the artiste's responsibility to know how to handle the microphone and the technicians' job to know how to get the correct sound that both the audience and the artiste want to hear.

Try to imagine that the microphone is the ear of a person and you are singing into that ear. When you whisper or sing quietly, the ear comes closer to your mouth. If you do any shouting the ear would naturally move well away from the sound and so on. There is always a 'happy medium' – you should use your intelligence and make adjustments all the time.

If you put your mouth too close to the mike, whatever sound you make is going to be over-amplified. More often than not this will make your words sound distorted, and there is very little the sound man can do about it. If the words are not important to you or your audience, then don't worry. 'Popping' can sometimes be a problem for first-time users, but can easily be corrected by you or your tech man. Singing at an angle, across, rather than full into the microphone, will usually cure it. Nevertheless, be careful when you have a song to sing with lots of p's in it – for instance, think of the song 'People', which in its first few bars has a plethora of the little 'poppers'. Popping can also be helped or even eliminated by a sponge-like cover, known as a windshield, which fits over the mike.

This little device is also a great help where sibilance is in abundance. Over-amplification or distortion of s-sounds can be disastrous, with the result of making you sound coyly lispy. A deadly example of this could be the Gershwin song 'S'wonderful'. Just be aware: using your ears intelligently will help you avoid noises that have no business being amplified.

If you intend to use the microphone both on and off its stand, it is of course necessary to remove it from its 'cradle' and to replace it as quietly as possible, otherwise you might create a clonking, thudding noise, a problem not easy to control, even for the experienced. Again, good technicians can help here, by dipping the sound, if they are told beforehand when you are going to do either movement. The safest way, I have found, after experimenting over the years with all the systems – the human being, the cradle and the 'butterfly clip' – is the last. It allows both operations to be performed swiftly and silently, simply by squeezing open the clasp that holds the mike in place. My road manager always has one handy just in case it's not available at the venue.

Extraneous noise can come from unexpected places. I learned this lesson when, during a sound check, my sound man, testing all his knobs and levers, was looking perplexed. When he was asked what the problem was he said: 'There's a ticking sound coming from somewhere and I can't find it to get rid of it! But I'll keep trying.' The culprit was discovered during a fast number, which brought about more head movement from me than usual, so in consequence my earrings were having a merry dance, jangling away noisily like castanets! The relief on his face was heaven to see – the guilt on mine fully deserved. 'Please – don't do that to me tonight, Cleo!' he said. The offending jewellery was put to one side for non-vocal occasions.

On the road again in the USA, with Mike Hatchard and John Dankworth

Loud breath-taking can be disturbing too, but if you can't do it silently, just turn your head away from the mike for the instant that you inhale. Some artistes feel that the breath is part of the instrument and should be heard, otherwise it would appear as though you were singing a whole song on one breath. If your breathing sounds as if you are vacuum-cleaning up every particle that is flying about in the air, merely to sing one phrase, then breathing and/or relaxation exercises are what you need.

For most amateurs and artistes starting their careers, a lot of this talk of microphones and amplification will be cloud-cuckoo-land, of course. Having the time and luxury of a long sound test is often out of the question – even a rehearsal is sometimes impossible. So it pays to find out as much information as you can when golden opportunities present themselves. When they do, ask questions and write down the answers for future reference. You should think hard in advance about how you want to sound and aim for it whenever you get the chance. Work with the sound man when it's possible, but don't accept out of hand his perception of your voice. It will save a lot of time, and you will, if your knowledge makes sense, be respected for it. Always get someone to walk around and listen on your behalf, not only from the back but the front as well – strangely enough, the front seats often present problems that are overlooked.

One last tip for the extra keen: observing the handling of the microphone by the best performers on a concert video is one of the simplest and cheapest ways to get a good lesson in its use and positioning. A caution here though: learn from performers but never copy their excesses or mannerisms. They may work for them, but it could be only because of their personality and stature in the profession. You will discover your own idiosyncrasies, as soon as you become comfortable with the extension of your voice through the instrument that is in your hand. If you try just a couple of my suggestions whenever you have an opportunity to grab the microphone, I am confident that you will feel much more professional and in control. It could add a new dimension to your performance.

I think it's time now to look into one of the most important needs of every singer, from beginner to professional. Whether the performance is in a grand opera house, a village hall, a cabaret room, a kitchen or a shower, the acoustics are crucial. Good acoustics ensure that the sounds the singers are making will carry and be produced with ease and with the least effort, giving the best possible results for their listeners. We all know the saying 'Yes, he's a great singer – in the shower!' Well, the magic that transforms the voice in the bathroom (maybe because of those tiles) is what, in a much more sophisticated and technical form, every acoustician in one way or another strives for. Yet the goal – of making the artiste on stage feel comfortable, sound good, and be able to achieve his or her full potential – is one that is often elusive, sometimes expensively so.

I discovered acoustics when I was living in a top flat in Kilburn, London. This was in the 'fifties. The block housed several well-known

British musicians, including the pianist Stan Tracey and the saxophonist Roy East. I learned a great deal about acoustics during my stay there – not from the musicians, but from my staircase. Acoustics, I discovered, helped voices either to soar, float and ring clear, or to fall flat at one's feet in a ball of cotton wool.

Getting up to and down from my London flat door was a daily workout not only for my body but also for my voice. I had to climb at least sixty concrete stairs, set in a lofty-ceilinged canyon of the same material. Each flat had a landing area situated outside its front door for easy entry, but I, the unfortunate top-flat dweller, sometimes had to use these areas to snatch a quick breath to continue my ascent. I was always very chirpy on my way down, realizing that if I sang it would give me a chance to warm up my voice for any future use it might have to encounter during the day or night. The sound on that stairwell carried the voice in a most remarkable and rewarding way. I managed to sing long phrases on one breath. I also found I could get much higher and lower vocally, and with more ease than ever before. Every day was a challenge to see how far I could get down the canyon on just one breath. I never managed a one-breath descent to the bottom, but it was a great way of warming up if I was on my way to a recording session or a gig. Going up was harder, but I was in pretty good shape at that time and could run up if I thought I heard the phone ringing in the distance. The going-up phrases were usually shorter though, for obvious reasons.

Everyone needs the help of good acoustics, from the great opera singers to the masters of popular song, either in a bright hall, with surfaces off which the voice can bounce and carry if you are a classical singer, or with the aid of a microphone if you are not. If the hall is dead and dry for some reason, everyone benefits from a touch of amplification.

Of course, performances in open-air venues almost always need microphones, as even the biggest and most highly produced vocal sounds would have difficulty competing with, say, a full orchestra or a traffic snarl-up just outside the performance area! There are exceptions, like the remarkable acoustics of the famous Caesarea amphitheatre in Israel, but in general, voices do not carry well without walls, preferably of a reverberating substance such as wood or brick – or a handy canyon. If, on the other hand, a hall is too 'lively,' the problem could become what I call a 'swimming pool sound': a vast, echoey noise where nothing is defined and lyrics become unintelligible. In these venues, all the sounds swim around together, and anything percussive takes over completely, often echoing several hundred times after a note has been played. I exaggerate, of course, but not much – it certainly feels like several hundred!

Places with 'over-bright' acoustics are a nightmare to perform in, as they are impossible to control, even if the accompanists play as quietly and with as much discipline as they know how. When they have to do this, it generally means that a certain amount of energy, life and 'balls' are lost from the music.

My staircase in Kilburn was perfect. I often wished I could have packed it up to use in all the famous places I have performed in across the world that have questionable acoustics. Over the years I have discovered and learned how to replicate the sounds I need from amplification, working with both good and bad technicians. Taking your own sound man on the road is expensive, generally a luxury only for multi-million-selling rockers on world tours (compliments of their record companies) or for promoters of mega-buck events. For many years I always used the same sound company when working in Britain, and they invariably employed technicians with good ears who understood my needs, even when I groped in the dark using non-technical terms for things I wanted to hear. When things started to sound right and to my satisfaction, I always made a point of finding out what magic they had worked – and in their language – so that I could try and achieve the same in the future, wherever I might be in the world.

If you want to be in control of what you are doing on stage, you and your musicians should do your darnedest to achieve a good internal balance, making sure that no one is standing out if he or she is not the soloist at any given time. If a musician fails to do this, the sound technician may well try to balance the ensemble himself – and unless he knows the music as well and intimately as the musicians do, it could spell disaster, with solos being missed and instruments jutting out when they have no business to.

If it is not used or handled correctly, amplification can give sound-assisted performances a bad name. Once again, ears are important – yours and the sound technician's. If it is at all possible, he should be given a chance to use his ears, by being allowed enough time to assess the hall in relation to the sound that is coming from the performance area. I can understand the complaints and grouses audiences sometimes have about amplification. However, often it has nothing to do with the technician but may be caused by lack of co-operation from artistes, venues that have not been designed for any kind of music, or by poor equipment that has been built into halls that were not intended to cope with any kind of amplification – the list is endless.

Overpowering sound can do much damage to a performance. The volume of sound should always be carefully judged, no matter what kind of music is played. But of course, in some cases, taste is a defining factor. To most heavy rock aficionados, 'loud' is an integral part of the music; certain instruments must stand out, such as the bass lines and the drum's pronounced beats. This would not suit or please an audience who enjoyed, say, a gentler volume of performance – as in folk music, show tunes or art songs.

Many styles of music cross over into each other's territory today, using the same instruments and sound techniques, and this often makes the sound technician another 'member of the group', with his all-round expertise of the music. Sound can then become another 'instrument', which is how a number of artistes today look upon it – indeed I have seen exceptional sound technicians given a bow after a performance.

Sometimes technology breaks down. What to do? Well, it's happened a couple of times in my career, once with a small group, in a small space. No problem there; just get the boys to rein in their enthusiasm for some of the numbers, and project my voice more. The other occasion, and more recent, was with an orchestra in a vast space. I had performed a concert at Carnegie Hall with the New York Symphony Pops Orchestra, under the direction of Skitch Henderson. It was a wonderful event that we all enjoyed very much. We were then scheduled to appear later at a university on Long Island to perform the same programme.

It was in the autumn, and an unusually big thunderstorm hit New York and the environs. The heavens opened, and we were driven to the venue in monsoon conditions, thunder and flashing lightning illuminating every slow mile of our journey. The windscreen wipers became a metronome that did nothing to help the visibility of the driver, who was no Speedy Gonzales before the thunder storm broke. He proceeded slowly and with much caution. We sang songs to the beat of the wipers.

Eventually we arrived, thankful that we were all in one piece. We dashed into the comfort of the backstage area, where I was allotted a small dressing room. The orchestra, who were there when we arrived, had to fend for themselves backstage. They were getting their instruments out of cases and starting to tune up to do their practice runs when the whole place was plunged into darkness. We presumed this would be a temporary glitch, and all would be brightness and light again in a short space of time. Candles and torches were produced from nowhere, while stagehands, lighting and sound technicians went to work, searching for the one switch that would illuminate us all and bring back the missing sound. Their search was in vain. Eventually the message came through that they could get only working lights going. Sound and stage lighting was dead for the evening, as several trees had collapsed on the main power circuits all over the district and it was highly unlikely that they would be repaired in time, or indeed that night. We all made the most of it. I and the ladies of the orchestra made up our faces and dressed by candle light, and wondered if the concert would be cancelled. But they decided that as the audience had made the effort and was a very respectable size for such a ghastly night, we should at least explain the situation, then give an unlit and unamplified performance.

The orchestra went on and played the first half, conducted by Skitch, in the half light. Then the real test came for me. It had been hoped that they might get sound by the second half. They had worked hard on it, but had not succeeded. Would it be possible for me to do the second half unamplified? I thought about it during the interval and said that if certain songs were cut, the ones with backings that were difficult to balance even with amplification, I'd have a go. It was not a small hall, in fact it was an arena, but the sound was bright. I knew JD would control the orchestra sound, as he was conducting for me. So during the interval we rearranged the programme, doing quite a lot with just my rhythm section. John also astutely cut passages that he felt would drown me. I had to produce a different singing style, of course, to get over and across the vast area, a style that is not my all-time favourite way of performing, as lower nuances have to be abandoned, and the higher register produced more and used most of the time, which does not make for light and shade in my performance. I use the microphone as if I'm playing an instrument, and the songs and keys are chosen in the knowledge that a microphone will enhance them and some of the notes that I will sing. Luckily, I have enough power in certain keys to perform without, as I had to in musicals such as *Valmouth*, *Boots with Strawberry Jam* and *Showboat*, all of which had foot mikes only, coming long before the development of the body mike used in all musicals today – quite rightly I think, as eight performances a week in a long-running production without such an aid, and singing at full tilt, is more than most voices, even highly trained ones, can stand without having some trouble. Opera singers, the most trained of all, would not even consider doing, or be asked to do eight performances in a row, with or without aid. For me, it just changes the character of the voice or song that I have to sing.

On this occasion the audience was not disappointed, as we thought they might be. In fact, when things like this happen, audiences, like artistes, seem to rise to the occasion, getting carried along with the circumstances, egging the artistes on and supporting them. We are all in this together – it's an event to be remembered – let's make the most of it. It is an experience that I can live without most of the time though, like camping out.

12

CARE OF THE VOICE

'Fresh air I consider the best tonic for the voice.'
                                                    Amelita Galli-Curci

Voice problems can strike at any time. The more you understand about the vulnerabilities of your voice, without making a big issue out of it, the fewer headaches you will get. Nothing can be as tedious as listening to a singer who has endless voice problems that they can't solve, if you are not their voice teacher, specialist or psychiatrist. The reasons that voices pack up, whether you are a professional or amateur, talker, singer or actor, are various and many. Just too much loud conversation at smoke-filled parties, can leave one voiceless the next day.

If you do any professional work regularly, you should seek out the best, most sympathetic voice specialist in your area and try to get to know him or her, if at all possible, before you have any need for specialist care. If you like the person, feel that you will be able to talk easily about non-vocal subjects, and sense that the feeling is mutual, then they are the person for you. Recommendations are probably the best way to find a specialist. Most artistes appearing in musicals have to visit one eventually, so theatres have either a list or one particular specialist to whom they send ailing voices to be repaired. If you have a friend in a show ask questions about their voice and whom they consult. They will be highly flattered and will love to talk about their precious instrument.

When I was in *Showboat*, before the winter struck hard and the flu season came around, in order to help protect the cast of a hundred performers, and their investment, the management provided flu jabs for everyone, including stagehands. It lessened the possibility of several artistes being out of action at the same time during the busy season that led up to Christmas, and the few months afterwards – the one time of the year when many theatres are able to make up box office deficits with a well-attended pantomime.

Flu jabs don't always work, however, so there are always artistes who will carry on no matter how they feel. I have done it myself, but I don't approve of it because you are spreading the germs among the company, and a lot of damage can be done, not only to the voice, but to one's health in general. Being fanatical about looking after a voice can be just as ridiculous as feeling the show must go on, no matter what. Common sense and knowing your instrument's needs and foibles are the guides you should follow.

It's not only physical problems, from strain to allergies, that can play havoc with a voice – emotional upsets can also have a profound influence. Emotional problems – from the most trivial to serious confessions, from the menopause or periods, to problems with boyfriends and girl-friends, and dissatisfaction with work – can affect the voice badly. When I have gone through difficult times in my life, my voice has suffered. There is such a direct connection between the voice and emotion that one's expressiveness can be severely affected.

I have spent many hours during courses for singers listening to the troubles of the students, young and old, before a note was ever sung. I realized it was important to do this, because of the benefits I had experienced myself when my teacher was on the receiving end. Whenever I needed a sympathetic ear to work through any of my problems, my singing teacher Madame Ertle listened, and we talked, instead of having a lesson. So I tried to do the same. I listened, and offered sympathy where needed, until I felt it was time for singing and work. It aided some and always helped to relieve tensions. A singer needs a good understanding listener (I mean listener, not advisor – that's for expert counsellors) for those moments when everything seems to be going haywire, and if you have one, treasure him or her. A little understanding, or a shoulder to cry on, can help you to sing really well.

I am often asked by non-performers the world over: 'Where do you get your energy from?', 'Don't you miss your beautiful home?', 'Aren't you tired of the constant travel, hotels and aeroplanes?' But the questions that crop up time and time again from concerned fans and friends are: 'How do you protect your voice with all the travelling you do?',

'What happens if you have a cold?', 'Do you have any secret rituals that get you through?' 'Well, no, I don't,' I reply. If it's working for me, I don't even think about my voice. If I have a cold, I can usually sing around it. But if a virus strikes, I have no solutions, no secret potions, and I'm in trouble, real trouble, if I'm working. If I'm not, I go and see a voice doctor and hope he'll get me straightened out by the time the next engagement comes round.

But it gets harder and harder to find a good, sympathetic witch doctor who will magically get you ready for the next performance, without using harmful medicines that are not suitable for a singer's throat. I did have two masters once, a couple of eccentric artistes who cared for singers because they loved them. They both came from Vienna and they were both trained by the father of the one, called Alfred Alexander, who worked in London. The other was Mr Grabshied, who lived and worked in New York. They were possibly the last of the Viennese tradition, both dying in their eighties, leaving opera, Broadway and West End stars quite devastated.

Between them, their waiting rooms were a veritable 'Who's Who' of the singing world. Alfred Alexander wrote learned books on the voice and singing, played the violin (well enough to be spotted in the orchestra of a West End musical), wrote songs, and was a lovable friend. Mr Grabshied collected glass, which is now in the National Museum of New York. He bred and loved Alsatian dogs, and spoke like Louis Armstrong with a Viennese accent. It made one's voice ache to listen to him talk. I often felt his love of training dogs came into his throat inspections, for he would stand at his door, which opened on to the waiting room, call your name and then command 'Come!' I have seen grand divas – stars of Broadway and cabaret – rise and enter then. Once inside the inner sanctum, without saying a word (after 'Come!'), he'd command 'Sit!' When you were settled in the leather swivel chair, the next command would be 'Open!', and then the magic began.

He also became a lovable friend. When I was appearing in *The Mystery Of Edwin Drood* in New York, I paid regular visits to him during the run of the show. Many a time he got me through difficulties with what I called his witch doctoring. His list of 'no-no's' every visit, delivered with a thick Viennese accent, was: no dairy products, no red wine, no chocolate, no tea. Although I am not, to my knowledge, allergic to these foods or drinks, it would never enter my head to touch any of them now when I had a heavy singing schedule. These two men understood not only the voice but, more important, the mind of a singer in distress and how it could work to make things go wrong. Singers the world over miss not only their expertise, but their friendship, too.

If you are aware that certain conditions affect you, you should prepare for them, avoid them, or seek help from a specialist for ease of mind. Next door to the Imperial Theatre in New York, where I was appearing in *The Mystery Of Edwin Drood* was a restaurant, considered by many to be the watering-hole for artistes appearing on Broadway. So, along with my co-worker and close friend George Rose I regularly ate there during the run. There is an American delicacy that comes into season once a year, namely soft-shelled crabs. They are quite delicious, and you literally eat the whole thing. Crab in the UK was never high on my list of 'must have' foods – like lobster, I always thought it was too much like hard work to eat, with all that nutcracker work to negotiate. But when I was introduced to this little devil, I fell in love. It was in this restaurant that I partook of my first bowl of this annual delicacy. I had no idea at the time, but these little sweeties turned out to be the Achilles' heel of my throat and vocal cords, causing them to swell. They played havoc with my voice, and I started to have trouble that I could not account for.

The allergy to crabs became known for sure when I ate some, oh so tasty, crab cakes, cooked to perfection by the chef at the Robert Mondavi vineyard, before a performance at the winery. All went well until towards the end of the concert, when my voice started to seize up. I just could not understand why it was happening. I went for a note and nothing came out. During the applause, I managed, out of the corner of my mouth to half-whisper, pleadingly, to John: 'Please, no encores, my voice is going'. Luckily he had noticed that something was wrong and that I was in trouble. He brought the concert to an end. The next day my voice was back to normal, virtually recovered. I had discovered the culprit, so crab in any form is now added to Mr Grabshied's list of 'no-no's' – with the one difference, that even when I don't have to sing, crab never enters my mouth. Many people are allergic to seafood, and singers should be aware of it. It certainly pays to find out what foods might cause blood vessels to swell, in case you are, or could become, allergic. It

Producing a good high note

has been found that peanuts can cause an allergic reaction that can be fatal for some people. But who would eat nuts before a performance?

So what does a performer do when far from home, on tour in Britain, or, in some cases, when at home? Voices do need special attention when things go wrong. Unless you have a regular specialist, going to your doctor for help can be frustrating for a singer at times, as some of the medicines prescribed will often make the problem worse – for instance, medication may dry up natural moisture, some cough mixtures contain alcohol, and much more.

There is an organization called the British Performing Arts Medicine Trust (BPAMT), which was founded in 1984 to carry out research and treatment in medicine for performing artistes. This is not exclusively for singers, and is open to musicians and dancers too. The head office and clinic are in London, and the organization has a nationwide data base through which people can be quickly referred to medical experts in conditions peculiar to the performing arts and their needs, within a given area or region. The association also issues a very interesting and informative booklet to members, reporting on current performing arts medicine and other related methods such as homeopathy, the Alexander Technique and many other interesting aspects. BPAMT was, of course, designed for professionals, but knowing that it exists could also be a comfort for an amateur with a vocal problem. At the end of the book you will find a list of addresses and telephone numbers which could be of interest or help, and BPAMT is included in this.

Section VI

A Personal Perspective

13

A MUSICAL BACKGROUND

Although this is a book about your singing voice, and how to free it, I thought it might be of interest to you to hear more of my own musical experiences. I hope in the process to be able to answer a few of the questions most frequently put to me at concerts and courses. Near the end of the book there are some more answers to frequently asked questions for you to dip into.

The question I have been asked most often of all by students and concert audiences has been 'How and when did you know that you were going to be a singer?'

Me on the right, with my brother Alec (left) and sister Sylvia

The answer is that I was lucky. I was born into a musical family, and I was able to develop the musical talents that had been handed to me in the birth lottery. It does not always follow that if a dad sings and a mother plays a little church organ, their offspring will have the desire to do the same. But it does give you a head start if you enjoy and want to join in the music that fills and surrounds the family home. In those days there were not so many diversions to take your attention away from any musical interest you might have, which was just as well, because developing that interest could help lead you out of poverty and struggle in later life.

We could not be a family of watchers or listeners, as so many are today. Although radio, films and concerts were there to be enjoyed, only radio was immediately available, unless you had the ready cash handy to satisfy a spur-of-the-moment desire to catch a concert or a film. Thus, like so many families of the 'thirties, the Campbell family entertained themselves. We all had a special song or dance that we honed and polished to get the applause of parents and friends at weekends – often, I'm sure, boring the pants off them, especially in the case of the other brother or sister waiting in the wings. My father also had the perfor-mance urge. As I wrote in my autobiography:

> My father had an excellent singing voice, and he loved to air it at any opportune moment, often embarrassing his children, his wife or anyone close at hand with his sudden vocal outbursts in the street, on the tops of buses, in the cinema queue or along with the performer up on the screen – when I at least would cringe and slip further down in my seat, pretending I was not with him. As we all had to leave together at the end of these humiliations, I wasn't very successful with my pretence. Everyone knew it was my dad who sang at the drop of a hat – anytime, anywhere. So I eventually came to terms with it, knowing he would never change. And I loved his singing, anyway, at home! He would sit us (two at a time – sometimes he managed three) on his lap and sing all the current songs of the day, from Al Jolson to Bing Crosby.

As all my names (Clementina Dinah Campbell at that time) happened to be song-titles, I claimed the copyright to sing them all by myself. No one else in the family could touch them in my presence for fear of their life. The songs were 'Oh My Darling Clementine', 'Dinah' and 'The Campbells are Coming' – three songs that I really put the enjoyment mockers on, in my family, for ever – even now when they hear them they groan. It might explain why, these days, I love to change my repertoire continually, for fear I might see eyes (between long-suffering ears) rise up towards the heavens, appealing to the powers that be: 'Oh please!! Not again!'

Looking back on my up-bringing, I would say that, if it hadn't been for the fascination in our family for all things musical, I'm sure I would have turned out to be an illiterate delinquent. I had no interest in working at school for most of the lessons. But reading was essential, to understand the written instructions for my early singing lessons, to read new lyrics and to try to read music at the same time. Again, although maths was never my strongest or favourite subject, I had to learn enough about the subject to count bars of music; I would have looked a lemon in class if, when singing, I had come in too soon or too late. So without music, I would not have acquired a basic education.

Indeed, more than a basic one, as I learned a lot of Italian, some French and German – and biology, via breathing lessons. That might be pushing it a bit, but I didn't do too badly. Because I loved music so much, I studied things I had no love for, in order to enjoy my passion even more.

Some of the enthusiasm I had for those early lessons at school was induced by the music teacher at the junior school in west London. She not only loved music, but showed the same love and devotion for teaching music to young children of varying capabilities who had very little besides music to brighten their lives – it was not the best of times for the country or that area. Our teacher managed to get out of a pretty motley crew of scruffy, snotty-nosed snifflers a creditable choir, and an annual concert that many a school today would love to be able to produce.

I can remember the sounds and songs that we sang in the assembly hall, getting ready for the parents' end-of-term concert or a celebration of a royal birthday – anything to get that choir working to keep it on its toes. At its best it made a glorious, full-throated, joyous noise. 'Nymphs and Shepherds, come away, come away.' A more unlikely looking lot of nymphs or shepherds you were never likely to meet. 'In these halls, in these halls we work and play, we work and play, we work and play, for this – this is Flora's holiday, this is Flora's holiday, this is Flora's HO-O-O-LI-I-DAAY!' That was about it – we worked and played, without bothering to find out who Flora was and why she was having a holiday, or that the music was by Purcell with words by Shadwell. The piece has stuck after all these years, as I still find myself breaking into the anthem of my childhood for no other reason than that it has come to mind and that it is a joyous thing to do. It amazes anyone in earshot. When I explain, they sigh pensively, saying: 'Oh yes, that was when they taught children music in schools'.

This teacher was knowledgeable not only about vocal techniques, but also in the art of gently nursing young voices into singing, without pushing them beyond their limits. I was really lucky to have been her pupil, as I had a tendency at that tender age to show off in an unforgivable fashion whenever I was asked to sing. And my idea of showing off was to sing as loudly as I could, with a chest voice that was not very pleasing to the ears – particularly if the song happened to be a lullaby. I had no taste whatsoever – I just sang everything loud. In fact, they called me Sophie Tucker, after a popular singer of the day. But they did her a disservice: the only thing we had in common was a very low voice.

I must admit I identified with – and was fond of – singers who had this low register, so it was only natural when I was young to emulate them. At the age of nine or ten I had an uncommonly deep, low voice – my natural register, a contralto. But, of course, if I had gone on singing the way that I was, without a gentle hand reining me in when I went over the top, I doubt if I would be singing today. I was heading in the direction of abuse of the vocal cords, but was checked by my teacher, and by the admonishments of my pa to 'belt up' and sing properly – in the nicest possible way, of course.

Here lies the danger that befalls many a would-be singer. I was never told to stop singing, but to sing better, and safeguard the lovely equipment that I had been given. Unlike me, my father and teacher were becoming aware of what was lying in wait for me, within my very young body and throat, and it was their duty to nurture it. In retrospect, they were the ones who set me on the right path, instilling in me at a very early age the need to protect my gift for the future. They were my mentors, the ones who, unknown to me at the time, gave me guidance and the confidence to take my first musical journey gently, carefully – and one step at a time.

14

BREAKING INTO THE PROFESSION

Another question that is often put to me is 'How did you break into the profession?'

'Break' is not a good description of my eventual entry as a professional singer – it was a much slower process! Before I eventually passed my umpteenth audition, I had worked as a semi-professional with local dance bands, and sung in pubs. I had also entered several talent competitions, none of which I won. I was very inexperienced and didn't deserve to win, but I always thought I should have – cocky me, with very little expertise to back up my cockiness. As I wrote in *Cleo*:

When I'd sung in a pub, a talent contest or an audition, I was inevitably chucked on, out of pressure of time, ending in an embarrassing struggle to pitch the song by guesswork, while the eyes of other hopeful performers, also waiting to be thrown into the same hell, pierced my uptight back. While my heart beat loud enough to be in a rhythm section – if it would only do the right beat and stop missing them. On these occasions, only faith, hope and a little charity could help me out: faith in my ear, hope that it hadn't let me down, and a little charitable understanding if I had started too high, I would eventually hit the highest note in the song. Meanwhile, the pianist generally floundered around behind me, trying to find, by ear, if he had one, the key I had just picked out of the blue. Lack of time or the inability of the pianist to play in any other key than the song was written in didn't help, but more than anything it was the sheer amateurishness of the singer that was at fault.

I blush with shame when I think of what those poor musicians had to go through and why so few vocalists earned their respect.

Cabarets in Manchester

My first gig was when I was nineteen years old, for a Labour party dance, for which I earned the grand sum of one pound, twelve shillings and sixpence. But my real lucky star struck when I passed an audition that I felt I had no hope of passing. It was in 1951 and the audition was for the Johnny Dankworth Seven, in a jazz club in the West End of London. I sang for John Dankworth and the pianist of the group, Bill le Sage, who accompanied me. I'm sure that if I went for an audition today with only the knowledge that I had at that time, I would be kicked out and told to go and do my homework. I could not 'count in' properly, and had no idea of the keys in which I would sing my songs. It was lucky for me that a) they badly needed a singer, b) they had auditioned their heads off that week with no success so far, and c) my voice and style came closest of any to what they were looking for. The band played modern jazz, and they were considered the *crème de la crème* of the British jazz scene. I had started at the top, with no more idea about the music that they were playing than the man in the moon. I had an abundance of confidence in my innate ability and that was about all.

A duet with Tony Mansell

An early gig in a Northern club

Frank Holder and me singing 'School Days' with the
John Dankworth Big Band in the late 'fifties

More hair, older, and still going strong . . .

The door had opened for me, and I was willing to learn all that I could. But I soon found that 'innateness' was not enough, and I had better get my act together before they found me out and gave me the sack. So I went about it at every rehearsal, asking and getting answers from the musicians and Frank Holder, the other singer in the band. Having a notebook with the song titles that I was going to sing listed in it, complete with the composers' names, the tempos and the keys I sang them in – all this was a start, but there was much more to come...

'First comes the phone call...'

Sammy Cahn

In 1972, I had one of the most exciting breaks in my career. Norman Granz, a devotee of jazz, owned the record label Pablo, which was devoted to jazz and jazz musicians. My introduction to him was a phone call from him asking me if I would be his 'Bess' on an album of the Gershwin classic *Porgy and Bess*, with Ray Charles singing Porgy's songs. I didn't even stop to consider pros, cons, wherefores or what-evers. 'Yes,' I said, 'I'd love to.'

After the screams of delight had died down, he gave me all the details. Although I had just arrived home from performing in the US, it meant going back almost immediately to Los Angeles to start recording. All I had to do was get the keys of all the songs I had to sing sorted out and get them to Frank de Vol, who was going to do all the orchestrations; I also had to learn any songs I might have to perform that had escaped my knowledge of the work. Luckily, I had loved the music of this classic jazz/folk opera from when I first heard it in the 1940s, as well as single tracks on various jazz records and a stage production from the 'fifties, culminating with the great Louis Armstrong/Ella Fitzgerald recording. I already had a medley in my repertoire of all the best-known songs, including 'Summer Time' and 'I Loves You Porgy'.

So I was well prepared, excited and nervous as hell, but looking forward to meeting a musician I had admired from afar, first on records, and later performing with his band in concert on various London stages. On every hearing, Ray's unique style of singing and playing was a lesson in relaxed, swinging from the heart blues/jazz. And he gathered around him players and singers of quality to support what he wanted to do.

Ray Charles and me, recording *Porgy and Bess*.
I think I'm turning over his music – Braille, of course

Norman Granz did the same for this recording. The orchestra was a formi-
dable 'Who's Who' of jazz and classical musicians living in LA.

I was all ready to go, I'd packed my bags to fly off to the city of angels,
when I got another phone call, this time saying: 'Unfortunately, Frank de
Vol has suffered a heart attack, so we will have to cancel the recording
until further notice.' I of course commiserated with all concerned; my
thoughts and sympathy were with Frank and his family. Then it hit me.
'Well, that's the end of that. I almost recorded with Ray Charles in LA,
but that's the way the cookie crumbles.' Ten days later I was, to
everyone's surprise, in the recording studio singing 'Summer Time',
conducted by Frank de Vol, and sitting behind a screen duetting with
Ray Charles on 'I Got Plenty of Nothing'.

Recording is not my favourite part of performing, but these sessions
were so relaxed and easy it never crossed my mind to think about
anything else but the beautiful music that was being played, the fun and
the opportunity to be part of what was turning out to be a memorable
album. This was not a dream; this was for real. So was the style of
recording, for we were in the studio with this immense orchestra playing
as we sang, live. It was not a track already laid down, as is the mode of
most recordings today. Mistakes, if made by either singers or musicians,
had to be wiped and we started again, hopefully with all mistakes
corrected. It was quite a challenge.

The resulting record brought about Ray's appearance as a guest artiste on one of the shows that I had on ITV. Once again, we had fun and lots of rapport, recreating the music we had recorded together and getting to know each other a little better. Ray is a natural; he sings what and how he feels. But it wasn't always that way. He told me he had a great love and admiration early in his career for the singing of Nat King Cole, and tried to emulate his style. Of course it didn't further his career at all, being a carbon copy of this wonderful singer. It was not until he realized this was a 'dead end' approach and stopped doing it that he discovered his own voice and a style of his own. He stuck with it, things started to happen for him, and he hasn't looked back since. He is now a legendary performer.

During the recording for a TV show one of the new arrangements was giving me trouble rhythmically. I asked for the music so that I could count myself in. I didn't want to hold anyone up. But Ray said, 'Ah! just listen to 'em a couple more times, Cleo. You'll soon feel it natural.' He was right; but if time had run short, as it so often does with TV recording, I would have had to fall back on counting. Luckily we had the luxury of time on our side on this occasion, and on the next take I came in singing, relaxed and free as air – thanks to Ray's suggestion to use my ears.

Of course, a combination of reading skills and an innate feel for the music is the ultimate goal for most musicians, blind or sighted. With the advanced technology of Braille and computers today, reading music is a skill that can be acquired by most unsighted musicians. As I discovered when I recorded with George Shearing, he has all the latest machines to help him with his life's vocation now, but, like Ray Charles, he started with his ears and a great desire to play. Technology came into his life much later. George's sensitivity, combined with his magical, instantly recognizable touch, makes him a singular player of both jazz and the classics. Working with him, you almost feel or sense his ears talking to him, saying 'Yes, George, that's where the fingers should go, that's the shape you want to get that juicy chord you're after, that's it, luverly.'

It's not as simple as that, of course, just me getting a bit dramatic. Years of hard study go into the end result of becoming a consummate, masterly musician like George Shearing. George, like so many other musicians I know, has a quirky sense of humour and at any obvious opportunity injects it into his music. He is also a master of spontaneous punning. One of the reasons musicians get on so well with each other is their appreciation of each other's jokes. Very few, certainly in jazz, lack a unique and humorous way of expressing themselves or events that happen in their lives. On a first visit to the UK, George's American wife, Ellie, was impressed with all the grandeur when they stayed at a rather posh hotel in London and said: 'I think I'd better go out and buy myself a tiara, to go with all this.' George replied, 'You'd better hurry. There's a tiara boom today.' Ouch!

I have a fond spot for musicians and their humour, as do many entertainers. They don't suffer fools gladly, but are quite often fools themselves, especially great ones who are often also a pain in the butt. Ronnie Scott was walking about his famous club in London in obvious pain one day, when a customer asked: 'How did you injure your back, Ronnie?' His reply was: 'Bending over backwards trying to please Stan Getz.' Stan had a reputation for being a very difficult person to deal with, but was one of the greatest tenor players jazz ever produced. I learned a great deal from listening to players like Stan Getz, and many other classy musicians from all over the world, including those I have collaborated with, both on record or in concert. Whatever kind of singer you aspire to be, listening to the best musicians in your chosen field can inspire in many ways. The list is endless – control, rhythm, phrasing, breathing, inspiration, ideas. And when improvising skills are what you're after, the more great improvisers you study, the sooner you will get a feel for what style will eventually work for you.

Michael Emmerson was the artistic director of the Belfast Arts Festival in the 'sixties, and this is where we first met and worked together. When he moved on to create other British festivals, such as those at Newcastle and Westminster, there was always a festival date for me in the diary. We became close friends, watching, admiring and supporting each other's progress along the way. When he became the manager of the then relatively unknown but already great flute player James Galway, I watched with immense interest. As Jimmy's career took off, he became one of the first of many classical 'cross-over' artistes, his fame spreading gradually worldwide.

Important telephone calls can be missed – and often were before the hateful answering machine was invented. (Hateful maybe, but it has become part of the life-saving equipment of artistes, managers and agents, releasing one from the tedious waiting by the phone for that call that would seal a deal or clinch a contract to make you a star.) A series of phone calls, some missed when the dreaded machine was not switched on, started negotiations between Michael, James, John Dankworth and myself. There were many reasons why it wasn't an easy transaction. A first obstacle to be overcome when two artistes tour the world, and between tours are busy with other commitments, is that of finding space in their diaries when both are free at the same time. Another is misadventures. On this occasion it was one that overtook James – he was knocked down by a motorbike while he was out walking near his home in Switzerland, an accident which landed him in hospital to have his legs mended. So things were going to be delayed considerably from the point we had reached at that stage.

John D, accustomed to recording techniques that did not require both artistes to be present at the same time for a record to be made, forged ahead while Jimmy was bound to lie still in bed. He made a tape-recording of all the proposed tunes together with the sketches of the arrangements. He had played all Jimmy's difficult flute parts on his clarinet at a slow speed, then had the tape speeded up, which gave James,

Tuition for Bill Cosby and me – from John Dankworth in Las Vegas

unable to try them himself (or even move) in his hospital bed, an idea of how things would sound. After hearing the selection of tunes and sketch arrangements, James said, 'They're great! Let's go ahead – when I get out of here.' John got back to him via Michael to say that he would go into the studio and get the instrumental backings finished, and that I would do as much as possible. When James was mended he would add his flute parts and we'd fit it all together. He agreed, and the end result was wonderful. After many months of to-ing and fro-ing, the record 'Sometimes When We Touch' was finally finished and soared up the album charts. 'Sometimes When We Touch' more than described the whole process, as we were only together in the studio when we happened to be free at the same time – at other times we worked alone. We went on to tour together, touching audiences the world over, performing songs from the album.

At that time I was beginning to learn the flute for my own enjoyment, so I was getting a free lesson, listening to the master every night. He introduced me to his very first childhood flute teacher, Muriel Dawn, someone he had remained very fond of and close to. As she lived quite near to where I was living I was able, when I was home, to visit her for lessons. Our sessions always started with her pointing out to me the importance of breathing correctly, supporting in a relaxed yet controlled way the expansion of the rib-cage and lower abdomen. Then she demon-strated the most efficient way to hold the instrument, followed with the requisite long notes to warm up the flute and the novice's embouchure (formation of mouth and lip muscles). She would then introduce me to a piece she hoped might be within my technical ability. She got much satis-faction out of teaching me. Often she would exclaim: 'Oh! what a delight to teach someone who is musical!' There was a reason for this outburst of enthusiasm for such a beginner on the flute. At the time she was tutoring young boys at a local school once a week, maybe in the hope of discov-ering another Jimmy Galway, but for them, soccer came much higher on their agenda than music, let alone the flute. I sympathized and tried harder for her. I also kept her updated as much as one could with Jimmy's playing exploits, so my visits were a dual treat for her.

Playing the flute, albeit sporadically, improved both my reading and my ear immensely, so I will be eternally grateful to Jimmy Galway for the introduction to good music lessons.

15

TEACHERS AND ROLE MODELS

Now that you have learned the rudiments, you might want to find a regular teacher to help you develop your voice further. But it is important to find the right one, or your voice might not benefit – it might, in fact, be damaged.

I am often asked if I had the same range when I started to sing professionally. The reply always surprises them, as much as their assumption that I was born singing like I do now surprises me. It presumes I have not done any work at all since! The reverse is true, of course; I had an extremely small range at first – just about an octave, which was all down in my boots. When I first reveal this to students I'm accused of pulling their legs, but it really was the case. I started as a contralto (and I still am one) – low, breathy, husky, sounding 'as if I had lived', as one critic of the time put it – but none of it was truly under control. I smoked too much for my particular good, as my respiratory system had been weakened during my childhood, through pneumonia, diphtheria and an annual bout of bronchitis brought about by London fogs. So, unlike the few singers who do smoke and get away with it, I was not able to, not without a lot of effort and discomfort. I could never have been a successful opera singer, because of my breathy voice – not that I ever wanted to go in that direction – but I did want to sing, and I wanted to sing well, no matter what road luck took me down. It took a while to improve my range and get from one octave to four. The way I did this was to realize my inadequacies, decide what to do about them and put into action what I had decided.

Sitting on the bandstand nightly with the Johnny Dankworth Seven, experiencing the musicianship of the group to which I now belonged, embarrassed me into improving what previously I was quite contented with. I was now starting to hear things that I could not articulate vocally because of my tiny range. Some of the arrangements that were being done for me were in keys higher than I would have chosen, merely to add light and shade to the repertoire, because to sing a group of songs one after the other all in the same key makes for a programme that sounds dull and uninspired. So I was (unbeknown to me at the time) gradually being stretched. But when I discovered what was happening without my being consulted I realized that I had to do something about it too.

The obvious and most sensible thing to do was go back to square one and take more singing lessons. But I didn't want to be changed; I wanted to find someone who would improve what was naturally there in me, to expand the range without forcing the voice, and who would work on my breathing. I didn't want to become an operatic or classical singer, but I did want to learn how they looked after their precious voices. Madame Ertle came into my life at the right time, just when I needed her. I have often read and heard it said, 'When the student is ready, the teacher will appear'. This happened between Madame and me. I lived near the school where she taught, and walked in one day to find out what was what, met her, liked her, and talked about what my needs were. The main one was my wish to remain where I was – with the band, singing the way that I was singing – but I wanted to get better at doing it. Would she take me on under those conditions, I asked?

I sang for her – and my lessons started again. She believed deeply in Buddhism, and I learned a great deal from her. She was Hungarian, and had suffered and lost family and friends during the Second World War, yet she showed no bitterness. She was, in fact, a very gentle-natured woman, believing in mind over matter.

'Think about it long enough, meditate upon it and practise it, and it will come,' was her philosophy. She gave me many visual images to dwell on when I was aiming for a note I had decided in my own mind was not anywhere to be found inside my head.

Some worked, others made me laugh, but I tried them all. Tipping forward and up on to my toes when I wanted to get a higher note often worked, especially if I also imagined that the note that I wanted was centred between my eyes, and would come out of the top of my head. I had to hear the note in my head first, of course, and this was achieved by singing scales and arpeggios along with my teacher's accompaniment on the piano. Another image I found harder to work on, but I know has done the trick for others, was this one. Imagine a rotting fish being dangled under your nose – then go for the note, with your face all screwed up in a rather ungainly way!

Listening and memorizing was of the utmost importance during lessons with Madame Ertle. You had to be aware, conscious of everything happening inside you, remembering the sensations and positionings in the mouth and head (the sounding board) when a note was produced that was satisfactory to both teacher and student.

Soon it became second nature and the imagery was dropped – I obviously could not go on-stage pulling strange faces, at the same time rising up and down on my toes, with eyes looking inward at an imagined whatever-it-was between them which hopefully would escape out of the top of my head as a note! Ludicrous as it all seems now, a lot of this approach worked for me, along with the more conventional techniques.

But study didn't stop with her. I had seven other 'teachers' from whom I was learning a great deal, apart from the music that I listened to while I was at work. I joined with the band in many after-hours listening sessions, when we gathered together in flats all over London or in hotel rooms on the road. The latest records were produced and studied meticulously. It was a wonderful time for me – I was introduced to a wide variety of music and musicians and learned a great deal.

Role Models

I was lucky that I found people whose music-making I loved and could learn from.

The Dankworth Seven were all idealists about the music they played and listened to, so it was difficult not to be taken up and along with all that enthusiasm. I was present during the nightly discussions on the history of jazz, modern musicians they revered, older players and composers who had influenced their present idols and themselves, and who would never, in the opinion of my new-found friends, lose their power to influence generation after generation of musicians.

They were certainly right. The list remains: Duke Ellington, Benny Goodman, Louis Armstrong, Ben Webster, Lester Young, Count Basie and countless others. The good singers we listened to are too numerous to list here. But three ladies whom we all admired without question were

Backstage with Tony Bennett in Seattle, 1992 , and
(clockwise) with Frank Sinatra, Chick Corea, Mel Tormé

Billie Holiday, Sarah Vaughan and Ella Fitzgerald. There were quite a few male singers who hit the spot too. Along with the three women the men who stood out were Billy Eckstein, Mel Tormé, Joe Williams and Frank Sinatra. They were all part of my singing lessons; listening to all of them, men and women, I picked what I needed from each one and discarded the rest.

Listening to Sarah, Frank and Mel told me I had to sort my breathing out if I ever wanted to sing long phrases with ease. Ella made me study ease of delivery and seamless technique, as well as listening and learning by ear the accompanying arrangement. The four men, too, showed me that you had to be aware of what the arranger had done, as they obviously were. Singing without reference to what was going on in the arrangement or accompaniment could lead to some unpleasant clashing sounds. Billie Holiday taught me the importance of, and the drama in, the sung word.

So I was back at school. I had found a teacher I could work with, a teacher who didn't want to alter me, just to improve what I had and give me confidence to go for what I thought I lacked. It would have seemed quite ridiculous then if someone had said to me: 'One day you will either meet or work with every one of your "record" teachers in one form or another,' but that has indeed happened, with the exception of Billie Holiday, whom I never met.

There does come a time when you have to stop being a full-time student and go out and do it for real. But you never stop learning. Wonderful new things present themselves, continually, grabbing your attention, seducing you back to the drawing board. Not only in jazz, which has given me the most pleasure, but in all kinds of music; and also in art, literature, photography, dance and drama. I believe having even a sprinkling of knowledge about all branches of the arts will help strengthen your chosen subject of music.

QUESTIONS AND ANSWERS

Over the years, at concerts and in courses, I am frequently asked the same questions, by other musicians, fans and students. Some of the key questions have been answered in the main text of this book, but here are a few others which pop up regularly.

Q: How do you rehearse bands tactfully?

A: Always find out who the leader of the group is and introduce yourself.

If there is no leader, ask the pianist or the most experienced player to help you – even if you do know something about rehearsing, it doesn't hurt to ask for help to get something right.

If you know your arrangements by ear (many professional singers know them only this way) and can hear that something is wrong but are unable to pinpoint the actual notes or the culprit, stop the music and go over the spot again. If the same thing happens again, ask the musicians 'if they would mind looking at the parts to see if anything is wrong with them, as it doesn't sound right'. If you know your parts are correct (make sure they are!), they will usually soon play the right notes.

Most important of all – if you are working with a group for the first time, and without parts, find out if they know your material. Avoid obscure songs or verses, unless they all know them well. Standards are always the safest, but musicians cannot be expected to know them all off the top of their heads. You should know your keys, and how to count in your numbers. Talk about tempos and endings with the leader before you start rehearsal, so that he knows what you want. Then, if there are any problems, he can convey them to the others and, hopefully, sort them out for you.

And remember, you are a singer, and your instrument is your voice. The other members' instruments are whatever they are comfortable playing and have trained to perform on. When you are out front singing a song, you are the soloist. If, however, you are part of an ensemble, your voice should not stand out, as this would unbalance the music.

This should cover most situations. Musicianship, combined with tact and humility on your part, will take care of the loose ends.

Q: Is image important today?

A: 'We all need to be re-invented from time to time in our life.' Novelist Gwyn Thomas said that when he was called for make-up before appearing on a TV talk show. Today this applies more in the performing arts than ever before. If you do start performing, you should be aiming for an image that you feel expresses your personality, and one with which you're comfortable, as first appearances set the scene for what is to come, and are important to your performances. I advise all singers who ask this question, but are resisting it on the grounds that it has nothing to do with music, that they will have to work on their image eventually, so why not think about it now? If you are a slob, a clown, introvert, extrovert – whatever you may be – be it with style. Make the most of your assets if you are thinking of entering the music profession. If you have something to offer, an original image is a way to get your talent noticed in the competitive performing world of today.

Q: Is it necessary to be able to improvise to be a jazz singer?

A: I assume you are referring to what is sometimes known as 'scat-singing' – that is, performing wordless passages in instrumental style. If you are, the answer is: No, I don't think it is necessary to be able to improvise – but many do. If you are not comfortable with scatting, or are no good at doing it, why bother – unless you want a challenge? It is, after all, composing on the spot, which is not an easy thing to do. There have been lots of jazz singers who do not 'scat-sing'. The most famous one I can think of is Billie Holiday.

But jazz singing is identified by characteristics other than 'scat'. The basic quality required for a jazz singing style has more to do with the sound, and, perhaps more important, with the delivery of that sound. The voice does not necessarily have to be low or dark; there are many jazz singers with voices that lie in the higher register. The type of song chosen to sing, and the way it is phrased, is also indicative of the jazz style. But if you have an interest in scatting, listen to the great experts and study their methods, in the same way as most musicians today have studied their instrumental counterparts. Indeed, singers can learn a great deal from the improvisations of jazz instrumentalists, so study them too.

Q: If you have a hearing impairment, are you still capable of singing?

A: According to Evelyn Glennie, if someone is born deaf it is virtually impossible for them to sing in tune. Among those who have lost their hearing later in life, it is possible for some to keep their voices and be able to sing, depending on the degree of hearing loss.

Q: I would like to be a backing singer, not a soloist. What do I need to be able to do this?

A: The ability to read music is generally essential, together with a well-trained ear for harmony. Courses for beginners abound – contact Jazz Singers Network, The Royal Opera House Education Department, or the Wavendon AllMusic Plan (see Useful Addresses for details).

Q: I have great trouble singing the notes in tune after they are played on the piano, no matter how hard I try. Should I get my ears tested?

A: If you have worked hard at it and still have no success, I think it would be a good idea. If the test finds nothing wrong, seek out a good teacher who can patiently guide you through your exercises.

Epilogue

GOOD LUCK, ALL YOU NEW SONGBIRDS!

I have come to the end of my book, and not only have I enjoyed writing it immensely, but I have also learned and re-learned a great deal for myself, trying out the exercises, so that I would be able to describe to you more clearly what to do and how to do it. I do hope that when you finished reading you went on to practise the suggested routines, with the conviction in your mind that they would make you a better singer. If you kept to your routine regularly from when you began, that should be the result.

I have always firmly believed that everyone can sing, if there is a real desire and a commitment to do so – the same commitment that would be brought to bear on any other interest or hobby. Singing is one of the most natural things in the world to do. It is being discovered and cultivated once again all over the world; by thousands of amateur choirs; by the young, getting together to form their own groups; and by many other aspiring singers of all ages who every year, rather than sit on a crowded beach, search out a music course that has a class for beginners or non-professionals.

The book has therefore been written for you in particular – those of you who wish to gather up more information and to improve. I hope it contains answers to questions that will help start you off on the right path to singing, or better singing, because many of those same answers helped me. I have included a number of my own experiences, in the hope that some or all of them might also help you. But I must emphasize that nothing teaches as much as your own experiences can. So, please, don't just read, get down and do it – only this way comes success. If there were any explanations, answers, or anything else that left you needing further illumination after your first reading, be assured that if you review whatever puzzled you, several times if need be, the problem will eventually be solved. Don't ever be afraid to go back to the beginning – again and again. If something is not clear in your mind, you will not be able to move forward.

If you are a beginner, you should practise every day. If not, it depends on what you are doing, and at what intensity. For instance, if you are learning new material for a show, yes. If you work every night in a show or your own concerts, yes. But if you have time off, and you have worked hard beforehand, rest. Always start vocalizing at least a week before beginning to perform again after a lay-off. Keep that practice tape handy.

I sincerely hope that you have also been inspired to find your own true voice – a voice that you wish to hone and improve for your own delight. If this has happened, then writing my book has been worth-while. So here's wishing you good luck – all you new songbirds!

USEFUL NAMES AND ADDRESSES

British Performing Arts Medicine Trust
18 Ogle Street, London W1P 7LG
Tel: (0171) 636 6860

Jazz Singers Network
P.O. Box 14224, London SW8 4ZG
Tel: (0181) 853 4730
The JSN facilitates workshops, promotes singers' venues and runs weekly jam sessions and regular social events.

Practical Opera Weekends
c/o Royal Opera House Education Department, Covent Garden, London WC2E 9DD
Practical Opera Weekends provide a chance to find out how an opera performance is put together, and take part yourself. These are arranged from time to time. To obtain details of any forthcoming events, write to the above address.

Sing for Pleasure
25 Fryerning Lane, Ingatestone, Essex CM4 ODD
An organization set up to promote singing for young people without technical musical knowledge. It provides information on choirs, courses and repertoire.

The Tone Deaf Choirs
38 Oakdale Road, London E11 4DL
Tel: (0171)558 2930
These are choirs designed to show participants that there is no such
thing as tone deafness, only panic. They provide lessons which aim to
change the focus of the student; the ability to listen improves and the
pitch is corrected.

Wavendon AllMusic Plan
Milton Keynes MK17 8LT
Tel: (01908) 582522
Wavendon presents high quality courses for singers and musicians in
relaxing surroundings.